C000127158

1 MONTH OF
FREE
READING

at

www.ForgottenBooks.com

ISBN 978-0-267-79312-9
PIBN 10015852

𝕿𝖍𝖊 𝕸𝖚𝖘𝖎𝖈=𝕷𝖔𝖛𝖊𝖗'𝖘 𝕷𝖎𝖇𝖗𝖆𝖗𝖞

EDITED BY
A. EAGLEFIELD HULL
MUS. DOC. (OXON.)

EVERYMAN AND HIS MUSIC

THE MUSIC LOVER'S LIBRARY

A series of small books on musical subjects in a popular style for the general reader. Crown 8vo

Edited by A. EAGLEFIELD HULL, Mus. Doc. (Oxon)

Shakespeare: His Music and Song. By A. H. MONCUR SIME.

Short History of Harmony. By CHARLES MACPHERSON, F.R.A.M., Late Organist of St. Paul's Cathedral.

Music and Religion. By W. W. LONGFORD, D.D., M.A. (Oxon.).

Foundations of Musical Aesthetics. By J. B. McEWEN, M.A., F.R.A.M.

The Voice in Song and Speech. By GORDON HELLER.

Everyman and His Music. By PERCY A. SCHOLES.

The Philosophy of Modernism. By CYRIL SCOTT.

The Power of Music and the Healing Art. By G. C. ROTHERY.

Modern Pianoforte Technique. By SIDNEY VANTYN.

The Story of British Music. By CLEMENT A. HARRIS.

KEGAN PAUL, TRENCH, TRUBNER & CO., LTD., LONDON.

EVERYMAN AND HIS MUSIC

SIMPLE PAPERS
ON VARIED SUBJECTS

BY

PERCY A. SCHOLES

FIFTH EDITION

LONDON
KEGAN PAUL, TRENCH, TRUBNER & CO., LTD.
BROADWAY HOUSE, 68-74 CARTER LANE, E.C.

TO MY WIFE

THIS LITTLE VOLUME OF ESSAYS, REPRINTED FROM
Everyman, THE *Evening Standard* AND *The Music
Student,* IS

DEDICATED

*Highwood Hill,
Middlesex.*

CONTENTS

viii CONTENTS

EVERYMAN AND HIS MUSIC

I

AN INTRODUCTORY CHAPTER

THAT in every age and in every place Everyman
has made music is a simple truth that admits of
no denial. Whether he live in a palace or in a
slum, his hours of recreation demand its help—
Beethoven and the barrel-organ are but differing
manifestations of the same desire to float away
the cares of life upon the wings of tone. Everyman's moments of religious contemplation call for
organ and choir; the bringing in of sinners is best
accomplished (so specialists tell us) to the accompaniment of the brass and the big drum. The
children playing in the market-place have their
piping and their dancing, and the greybeard is
young again as he listens to the songs of his youth.
Everyman makes war and he joins in marriage to
the sounds of music; his earliest toy is a rattle,
his next a trumpet, and his passage to the grave
has its own traditional march.

It is the great thinkers of every age who have

B

most clearly seen the power of sound. Plato made claims for it that the modern musician (with his vastly more complex art than Plato ever knew) would not dare to extend. Milton allowed it " a great power over disposition and manners, to smooth and make them gentle from rustic harshness and distempered passions." Wordsworth shows us the street fiddler as a modern Orpheus; Burton reminds us that music is the art that can make " a melancholy man merry, and him that was merry much merrier than before, a lover more enamoured, a religious man more devout." Old Sir Thomas Browne, as befitted a man of his profession, begins with a physiological metaphor : " It unties the ligaments of my frame, takes me to pieces, dilates me out of myself, and by degrees, methinks, resolves me to heaven." ·

Some few there have been, it is true, who have professed to live beyond the reach of music's sway, but their profession was more or less make-believe. Johnson asserted to Boswell that he was " very insensible to the power of music," yet he once tried to learn the flageolet (" A flageolet, sir ! " says Boswell, " so small an instrument ? I should have liked to hear you play on the violoncello "); and when they " had the music of the bagpipe every day " at Dunvegan " Dr. Johnson appeared fond of it, and used often to stand for some time with his ear close to the great drone " (though this, perhaps, may be thought a doubtful proof of musicality). Lamb gave it out : "I never could be made to understand (yet have I taken some pains) what a note of music is, or how one note should differ from another "; yet he loved to haunt the house of his " good Catholic friend,". Novello, " who, by the aid of a capital organ, himself the most finished of players, converts his drawing-room into a chapel, his week-days into Sundays, and these latter into minor heavens."

Music is, in fact, for *Everyman*, and when the cry, " Great Pan is dead," rang through Nature, and the old world gave place to the new, Pan's art lived on, still lives, and ever will. The syrinx and the nymphs who danced to it faded away, but the Prodigal Son of the Parable was welcomed with " musick and dancing," and in the Interpreter's House the master " did usually entertain those that lodged with him with music at meals." Now the modern folk-dance movement has set the nymphs afoot again, and every modern restaurant has taken a leaf out of the Interpreter's book. These things never die. Music is not merely a matter for the cultured; it is inextricably bound up in the bundle of common life. It is born in Everyman *to need* music.

II

"BAYREUTH," says Hermann Bahr (than whom nobody knows it better), "has nothing in common with the infamous 'everydayness' of our civilisation." In *The Nation* lately, Mr. Francis Toye was up in arms against the implication involved. "Art," he says, "is become a luxury, and musical art a very expensive luxury, instead of a necessity for every normal educated human being." The most pressing need of modern times is "to bring the conception of the artist as primarily a craftsman back into common use." In Italy, in the greatest period of pictorial and plastic art, "the painter, the sculptor, and the worker in metals were regarded in very much the same way as we regard the workmen who decorate our houses." "Art" and craft, I suppose, according to this view, may be said to have applied for a divorce and got it; the former has gone up in the social scale, and spells its name with a big "A," whilst the latter has gone down, and uses a very small "c." Instead of ministering to the everyday wants of the plain men and women of the world, the "Artist" is out for hero-worship.

Beethoven and Wagner must shoulder the responsibility for all this, Mr. Toye thinks. They proclaimed their right to a complete expression of their personality, never dreaming that their followers, to achieve this admirable ideal, would claim exemption from the ordinary musical routine of the day.

Mr. Toye is not the first to express opinions of this kind. Mr. Bernard Shaw has anticipated him in the engaging *Reminiscences of a Quinquagenarian*, of which he made a present, a few years ago, to the learned members of the Musical Association. There he exclaims that there is only one place to-day where the craftmanship of music may still be cultivated—the theatre. "In the theatre," he said, "if I want a piece of music of a certain length I can get it exactly that length. If in the course of rehearsal I want it altered to suit some change in the stage business of my play, I can get the alteration made. The conductor does not say that his inspiration cannot be controlled in this way, and that he must work his movement out as his genius prompts him and as its academic form demands. He does not tell me that he cannot do what I want without eight horns and four tubas, half a dozen drums and a contra-fagotto. He has to do it with one oboe generally. He is really master of his materials, and can adapt them at a moment's notice to any set of circumstances that is at all practicable. And it is precisely because he can do these small things when other people want them that he can do great things when he himself wants them." And Mr. Shaw adds that in the days when he practised as a musical critic the greatest master of orchestration in London was—the musical director of Drury Lane.

Now, in all cases of doubt as to the principles of art the appeal must be to history. And in this instance the decision (up to a certain period, at all events) is plain. Palestrina contrived masses that met the ideals of a Pope and a Council. Purcell wrote stage music very much in the way Mr. Shaw describes, and became an adept at the fashioning of anthems that should be sung at one and the same time to the praise and glory of God and the diversion of a light-hearted king. Bach, in the pay of a town council, was occupied week after week in turning out Church cantatas suited to the varying needs and resources of a small choir and insufficient orchestra. He made two hundred in all—more than the average musician of to-day can hope to bring within the range of his bare acquaintance. Haydn manufactured one hundred and twenty symphonies to the order first of a prince, who employed him in his palace for the purpose, and then of a London concert agent, who commissioned them half a dozen at a time. Mozart worked for the pleasure of a royal archbishop, and, later, to the plans of a theatre manager. These men, then, were masters of their craft. The days of hero-worship were not yet. People asked a musician for what they wanted, and he was tradesman enough to supply it. Like Shakespeare, he undertook a commission as hackwork, and (in a proportion of instances, at any rate) turned it out a masterpiece. "There is nothing paralysing to musical invention in writing to order or for money," says Mr. Toyé, "so long as the composer is not expected to lower his own standard of taste in the process."

The great point of all this, of course, is that if the public are to call for what they want they V must be taught to want the right things. Better, as most would say, that the composer should starve on the composition of symphonies at the moment too good for the public, than roll in his motor-car on the proceeds of sentimental anthems, drawing-room ballads, and weak waltzes. Mr. Toye, however, is heroic. He would "bring the composer and the people face to face." Rather than that the great gulf fixed between the artist and the plain man should remain for ever unbridged, he would have the former build out across it until he could join hands with the latter. " In plain words, I would like to see our most talented composers everywhere—in the organ lofts, writing services and anthems for their choirs, cantatas for the local choral societies, a string quartet or two for the best players of the district; in the conductor's chair of the theatre, producing incidental music for plays and, perhaps, small ballets, condescending, if their talents happened to have some kinship with those of Offenbach and Sullivan, to think kindly of musical comedy occasionally; briefly, in every musical situation conceivable, writing compositions primarily intended to satisfy the immediate requirements of their various offices." In fact, so to speak, Mr. Toye would, for a time at any rate, abolish authorship and substitute journalism (the idea of " everydayness " is etymologically implicit in this latter word, so it meets the case very happily). One may be far from agreement with such a whole-hogger as our writer appears to be, and yet see some truth in his final contention: " At present the whole structure of our serious musical life rests upon the most unstable foundation. It is practically built on a marsh, with the critical eclectic and the wealthy dilettante as sole supports. And unless we can grout it with the cement of ' everydayness ' we may at any time witness the most appalling collapse." " How long should or can any democratic civilisation support an art better than itself ? "

III

ENGLAND AS A MUSICAL COUNTRY

THAT England is to-day a musical country is a matter on which she herself has doubts and her Continental neighbours none. That she once was such is a fact beyond her questioning or theirs. That she is in process of again becoming musical is a cherished belief of some who profess ability to read the signs of the times. Let us first consider the glorious times that were, treading the safe ground of assured fact.

(1) Twelve hundred and twenty-six, or thereabouts. Henry III is on the English throne. A monk of Reading Abbey (one John of Fornsete, in all probability) composes the earliest piece of harmonised song that is to be still performed in the far-distant twentieth century—*Sumer is icumen in.* You can get a copy for 1½d. (Novello). Look at it carefully. At a period when Europe is still singing its beautiful old plain chant, either as simple melody or with the addition of a rude discant, this English monk has produced a delightful " canon four in one " (four voices with the same tune, but entering one after the other—treading on one another's heels, so to speak). Moreover, under it he has placed what

9

he calls a *Pes*, and what we call a " ground-bass " (a little piece of melody repeated over and over again), and has actually fitted this in canon also, for two voices.   Here is marvellous contrivance wedded to genuine beauty—a real work of art and one unparalleled in any other nation at this early period.

(2) We skip nearly a couple of centuries. Henry VI is King. Chaucer is not long dead. Soon they will be burning Joan of Arc. The art of combining melodies, hit on by accident by the monk of Reading, is now placed on the firm basis of a science by another Englisman, John Dunstable. His compositions are eagerly copied by monks working in quiet monasteries all over the Continent, and cathedral choirs everywhere discard their old crudities in favour of the new artistic style. Again, England leads!

(3) Nearly two centuries on again. Now Elizabeth reigns. English enterprise and English literature have reached high-water mark. Shakespeare and Spenser are at work. So are Raleigh and Drake and Frobisher and Hawkins. So is Bacon. And so, too, are a splendid group of musicians, such as Byrd and Bull and Dowland. These men are famous as performers and composers. Bull (let him have his full name, John Bull—English enough that!) becomes organist of Antwerp Cathedral; Dowland takes service as Court lutenist in Denmark, and his works are printed in Paris, Antwerp, Cologne, Nuremberg, Frankfort, Hamburg, Leipsic, Heid-

elberg, and Amsterdam. Byrd writes not only beautiful madrigals and church music, but also, with his fellow-English composers, lays the foundation of keyboard instrumental music—as Rubinstein and others are afterwards to admit. The English are still innovators.

(4) The later Stuart Period. In the year that Cromwell dies, Purcell is born. He becomes the organist of Westminster Abbey, the chief musician to Charles II, James II, and William and Mary, and the favourite theatre composer of the day. He writes in all the forms—songs, anthems and services, sonatas for stringed instruments, pieces for harpsichord and organ, stage choruses and overtures—everything. Above all, he has the gift of *melody.* Any fool can " compose " if he has proper teaching and a measure of perseverance; but a real "tune" is a divine gift. With Purcell, too, we see the beginnings of modernity in music, as with his contemporary and friend Dryden we see its beginnings in literature. His influence is, a few years after his death, to be felt by Handel (especially in the matter of choral writing). And Handel's *Messiah* is to prompt Haydn's writing of *The Creation*— and so English influence is to be carried forward even when England herself shall have lagged behind in the race (only for a time, let us hope!).

When England's musicality is questioned let us remember that our national pride can, at any rate, reach the end of the seventeenth century without a fall.

A Short Bibliography of English Music.—Some useful books on this subject are the following : Walker, *A History of Music in England* (Oxford University Press, 7s 6d.); Davey, *A History of English Music* (Curwen, 6s.); *English Music, 1604-1904* (Scott, 3s. 6d. net); Bumpus, *A History of English Cathedral Music* (Laurie, 2 vols., each 6s. net); Eaglefield Hull, *Short History of Music* (Messrs. Kegan Paul, 1s. 6d. in this series); Barrett, *English Church Composers* (Sampson Low, 2s. net); Naylor, *Shakespeare and Music* (Dent. 3s. net); Cowling, *Music and the Shakespearean Stage* (Cambridge University Press, 4s. net); Naylor, *An Elizabethan Virginal Book* (Dent, 6s. net); Van den Borren, *Les origines de la musique de clavier en Angleterre* (Groenveldt, Brussels, 1913, 5 fr.); English translation of the last *The Sources of Keyboard Music in England* (Novello, 7s. net); Cummings, *Purcell* (Sampson Low, 1s.6d. net.); Runciman, *Purcell* (Bell, 1s. net); Bridge, *Samuel Pepys, Lover of Musique* (Smith, Elder, 5s.); Galpin, *Old English Instruments of Music* (Methuen, 7s. 6d. net); Sharp, *English Folk-Songs* (Novello, 7s. 6d. net); Kidson & Neal, *English Folk-Song and Dance* (Cambridge University Press, 3s. net); Vaughan-Williams, *English Folk-Songs* (Joseph Williams, Ltd., 6d. net); Galloway, *Musical England* (Christophers); Antcliffe, *Living Music* (Joseph Williams, Ltd., 2s. 6d. net). This last has chapters on the subject.

IV.

OF CHURCH MUSIC

THE limited vision and the small mind are the crowning curse in any domain of life or thought. In Business they leave a man in his own back-street shop when he might be supplying his commodities to continents. In Politics they permit him to be a mere Radical or Tory when he might, in addition, be a humanist and a sociologist. In Religion they breed intolerance. In Art they are the responsible creators of passing fashions and brief antipathies.

These reflections (somewhat trite, perhaps) arise in my mind as the outcome of the reading of some words of Dr. H. Walford Davies, one of the sincerest spirits in the English world of music to-day. In these he shows us the main bearings of the subject of " Music in Christian Worship " (for that is his title*), and gets so near to *first principles* that a priest in the Greek or Roman Church might profit almost as much as the Protestant, and the Buddhist or Mohammedan would not be left without food for thought.

" I have heard art sweepingly described in the pulpit as a plaything," says Dr. Davies, and then

*Church Music Society (Humfrey Milford, 2d.)

goes on to condemn " the equally thoughtless extreme that puts music apart from all human affairs as a *divine* art." Music, of course, like all the Arts, is a means of human expression—but human expression under control. That, I suppose, is the true touchstone of music in all places and all ages. Bad music is of three kinds: (1) That which expresses nothing worthy, but expresses it well; (2) that in which the matter is good, but the manner of expression poor; and (3) that which has merits neither of matter nor of manner of expression.

" There is a recurrent human joy," our author tells us, " in the exercise of every natural faculty, from the obvious lowest to the dimly apprehended highest. Our faculties, our exercise of them, and our joy in that exercise are probably quite indivisible. For purposes of analysis, however, they are conveniently classified under the heads of sensation, emotion, reason; and above these is discovered the continual play of less obvious and, as we believe, more momentous faculties which may be grouped together as intuitional." Religion, as he points out, is concerned with the mysterious fourth order of faculties. " Its whole endeavour is to bring the known and seen into complete subjection to the unknown and unseen." Music is not only a " pleasing exercise " of the feeling and thinking faculties; it shows numberless signs of the great " fourth order." Wrong estimates of art in the past have arisen from partial views of it as decorative or emotional or sensuous. It is all these, at one and the same time, and, in addition, it allows a place (perhaps the most important place of all) for intuition, for " inspiration."

" One great use of Christian public worship is to formulate and communicate a superior order of life." Music is an innately suitable handmaid to worship precisely because she also seeks to formulate and communicate something free and joyous in terms of comprehensible orderliness. Moreover, she has a " fine power to hint," and the notes of an anthem may carry us further than the words.

All these are but a few thoughts actually stated in or arising from Dr. Davies' fine contribution to a discussion of a great subject. They may, however, be sufficient to provoke a useful train of thought in the mind of some church musician or lover of church music.

V

A DEFENCE OF THE CHORAL SOCIETY

"WHAT a caterwauling do you keep here!" said My Lady's servant to that "dog at a catch" Sir Andrew and his boon companions, Sir Toby and the Clown, as they made the midnight hours vocal outside My Lady's house. And that is very much what that most vigorous amongst London music critics, the late Mr. J. R. Runciman, was saying not long ago in the "Saturday Review."

From the days of Sir Andrew down to our own, choral song has been our chief artistic boast—the one thing musical that we prided ourselves on doing better than the best of the so-called musical nations; our strongest claim to fame since Charles II beat time to the anthems in the Royal Chapel, since Cromwell solaced himself with the motets of one Richard Deering, since Elizabeth, as the great "Oriana," figured as heroine of a multitude of madrigals.

Other peoples might have their orchestras and their opera houses and welcome—expensive luxuries rarely to be arrived at without the support of the subsidies, from state and municipality, which practical Britain has always withheld; we had our choral societies, bravely paying their own way, or at most calling for the same measure of monetary backing at the hands of the local M.P. and the other " patrons " as the local. cricket or football club. A democratic form of art is the choral society: not one man in a million can paint a picture, not one in a thousand can play the fiddle well enough to join in a string quartet; but fifty men, or more, in every hundred can, be they so disposed, " bear a part " (as Shakespeare would say) in some old masterpiece of Byrd, or some new one of Bantock. Why, then, is this long-time glory of our land to be condemned?

It is the war that has done it! As a result of diminished audiences and of the good work of the recruiting sergeant among the tenors and basses, some societies have ceased to sing. Many more continue than Mr. Runciman seemed to know about, but in any case his argument, so far as I could grasp it, was a little weak. The idea appeared to be: Choral societies have stopped; the world still goes on; therefore choral societies are superfluous!

But history, too, was called upon. " In the early part of last century," we are told, " choral societies had their uses. They sang the masterpieces of oratorio at a time when no other music could be heard." But they grew complacent, settled down to sing a few " standard " works, and allowed the artistic element to become " hopelessly and eternally alienated." Then came the day of the pot-boiler cantata, popular and easy to sing; " all good music was dropped," and, worst

c

of all, " in every suburb of London and any pro-
vincial town all the money available for music was
secured by these grotesque entertainments."

Now if Mr. Runciman never before strayed from
the straight path of fact, when he wrote these words
he had at last done so. It is known to the world
that if the word " progressive " can be fairly fitted
to any branch of artistic activity in our country
during the last decade or two, choralism can claim
the honour. In point of technique, the larger
societies, such as those of Sheffield, Manchester,
Bristol, Leeds, and Glasgow, have been tackling
works of a difficulty never dreamed of previously.
No composer previously has dared to write such
passages for the voices as Elgar and (especially)
Bantock have been writing. The result has been
a widening of the bounds of musical expression in
a wonderful degree. The Christian Gerontius and
the hedonistic Omar have equally found their
voice. (How could they have spoken in the choral
language of any previous period?) And whilst
the big societies have been revelling in works like
these, the smaller ones, stimulated by a hundred
admirable " competitive festivals," have been singing the modern part-songs that no composer knows
better how to write than the British.

VI

S AID Marshal Saxe, " The Romans were generally victorious *because they were made to march in time.* This is the perfect secret; it is the reason of the institution of marches, and the beating of the drum."

Now Marshal Saxe was no scholar. His famous letter declining the honour of election to the French Academy was the neatest piece of unconscious sarcasm, for almost every word in it was ludicrously mis-spelled. His information as to the Romans may therefore be discounted, but the view implied as to the disciplinary value of military music is a different matter, especially since he showed his confidence in its correctness by acting vigorously upon it.

Music and marching were associated in the minds of the Marshal and his contemporaries. The rhythmic value of music was what struck them. And so they modelled their music on that of the nation that has always made a large use of rhythmic instruments, and the Turk ruled Europe in the domain of military music. So came army bands made up of a few hautboys and fifes with an unconscionable deal of drum, cymbal, triangle

—and even tambourine. And the British Army, like the other armies of Europe, marched to the rattle and clang and jingle of all manner of instruments of percussion, including even that baby's toy on a giant scale, the "Jingling Johnnie," a rod whose crescents, hung with little bells, proclaimed its Oriental origin.

Beethoven's *Turkish March* in his *Ruins of Athens* probably gives a pretty good idea of a style of military music which seems to have persisted in some countries into his day, and the black bandsmen, who were a feature of our bands until the accession of Victoria, kept up the tradition that the star of military music rose in the East. The 2nd Life Guards, by the way, had some blacks in their band until just before the Crimean War, and so also had the Coldstreams and the Scots Guards. The present day muscular display of the drummer, with his sticks, as he swings them over first to one side then the other is a relic of the days when Oriental exuberance devised all manner of extravagant action, even to leaping and jumping before the regiment like David before the ark.

Nowadays our soldiers march to something better than mere rhythmic noise, and the model of the present-day bands may probably be found in that of the Royal Artillery, which was the first army band to win official recognition in the tangible form of provision in the Army Estimates. This was as early as 1742. A German influence had already begun to displace the Turkish, and a quite artistic combination was found in **two** trumpets, two horns, two bassoons, and four oboes or clarinets. Moreover every bandsman was required to be proficient upon a stringed instrument also, and the " double-handed " condition of to-day was thus early laid down.

British musical modesty is nowhere more strikingly shown than in the fact that for a long time it was taken as a matter of course that bandsmen must be foreigners, and for a longer time still the tradition of the foreign conductor flourished. This very Royal Artillery band, for instance, had existed nearly half a century before a British musician first controlled it, and when, in 1810, the happy change came about, it was but by a strange fluke, for another half-century passed before the thing became general. Germany and Italy up to that date supplied us not only with our bandmasters but largely with our bandsmen. There are old soldiers living to-day who can recall the time when every regiment that *was* a regiment prided itself on its German bandmaster and its French cook.

Recently the King and Queen and 8,000 or 9,000 of their loyal subjects spent a pleasant Saturday afternoon's holiday in the Royal Albert Hall, listening to a massed performance of the eight bands of the Household Brigade. There are several interesting points to notice about this performance.

Firstly, one's eye is caught by certain names on the programme, and as one glances over them one realises how completely the foreign tradition has gone. For the eight bandmasters bear English names, like Miller, or Hall, or Bilton, or Wood, or Hassell, or Harris, or Welsh names, like Williams, or, in the case of the conductor for the afternoon, a Scotch-Irish combination in Mackenzie-Rogan.

Secondly, there is evidence that nowadays we are willing to spend money on the support of our military music. "But where are your 'hautboys?'" asked the King one day of Marlborough at a big review. The great commander's hand sought his breeches pocket and the rattle of money was heard. "Here they are, your Majesty; don't you hear them?" was the reply. That spirit has gone. The Army has its fine music to-day largely through its willingness to pay for it.

Thirdly, a sad thirdly, the programme shows that there is one laggard in the march to perfection of British military music, and that is—the British composer. That composer forgets his largest potential audience when he neglects to provide for these bands, which all the year round, indoors and outdoors, up and down the country, are nowadays playing not only to the officers and men of their regiments, but also to thousands of enthusiastic civilian auditors.

VII

A NEGLECTED FORCE—THE BRASS BAND

A SHORT time ago there came to me, for publication in a musical journal of which I am editor, a report of a meeting. It contained an amazing statement, credited to Dr. W. G. McNaught. Wishing, in the interests of the reputation of this well-known authority, as well as of that of my paper, to check its accuracy, I wrote to him on the matter, and his reply was still more amazing. The statement was this: "There are at least 20,000 brass band instrumentalists in the country." The reply to my query, if I remember rightly, was as follows: "I have made inquiries, and find I have underestimated the number; there are 20,000 *in the North of England alone!*"

The fact is, the average professional musician and musical journalist carries on his labours amongst the higher and middle classes of the country; the brass band is essentially a working-class possession, and he is apt to lose sight of it. Thinking it over, however, and recollecting the popularity of this social and musical institution in manufacturing and colliery districts, I realise that there is, after all, nothing so astonishing in the statistics given. Little as the cultured musician may recognise the fact, the brass band actually is one of the biggest forces in our national musical life to-day, and no feature of that life (except, perhaps, choral singing) is so bound up with the everyday existence of the mass of the population. I take it that the brass band is essentially the factory worker's and collier's musical activity, and recall with pleasure the part it played in the life of a little manufacturing community, happily planted not in a grimy town, but, for the sake of water power and cheap labour, in a lovely Yorkshire valley. "The Hope of Darley" was, I believe, the dignified title of this group of enthusiastic instrumentalists, and what the school feasts and cricket matches of the district would have done without its enlivening presence is hard to imagine. Three or four miles over the moors, in another little valley, there is a great ruined mill—the mute protest of a countryside robbed of its population that the great city thirty miles and more away might enjoy an ample and uncontaminated water supply. Here, on the walls of the roadside inn, hang the now silent, but still ever brightly polished instruments with which the vanished factory workers once made music under the skilled direction of the innkeeper himself. One can imagine in what a valuable artistic possession these simple labouring people rejoiced!

It seems a great pity that our young British composers, who are for ever grumbling that they cannot get publishers to print their works or audiences to hear them, should with one consent

ignore this great national form of music-making.
So far as my knowledge goes, the music performed
by wind instrumentalists is largely either rather
commonplace original work, or (more often) " arrangements " of music written for some other
medium. Opera is perhaps not one of our national
forms; a large portion of the community cares
nothing for it, and the chances of a hearing for
a new work are indeed slight in a country which
possesses only one real opera-house as against
hundreds elsewhere. But our composers go on
making an attempt which is well-nigh hopeless.
Orchestras are few, and must remain so, since
their organisation is an expensive matter. But
composers spend their days in writing orchestral
music, and if they get one single performance of
a piece have reason to feel themselves very lucky
indeed. And all the time, from thoughtlessness
or false dignity, they are ignoring an opening
which should not only prove remunerative, but
also give them a means of exercising a leverage
on our national musical taste which they can in
no other way effect. Moreover, in writing for the
brass band, they would be providing music for
the people whose lives most need it.

VIII

PURITANISM AND MUSIC

THERE was lately a merry dispute going on in the *Pall Mall Gazette* about English music. My friend Mr. Geoffrey Shaw seems to have started it by one of those uncompromising articles of his, in which he shows, as he thinks conclusively, (1) that there has been plenty of English music in the past; (2) that there is none in the present; (3) that there can be lots in the future, if only the English composer will adopt the English idiom, instead of trying to speak broken German.

Now all newspaper correspondence sooner or later strays into side tracks, and Mr. Athelstan Riley, who was one of the *Pall Mall* rioters, showed that he quite understood what was expected of him when he contributed to this vigorous and interesting discussion the following assertion :—

" Down to the Great Rebellion, English music and English composers occupied the very first rank. It was the destruction of that splendid school by the sour fanatics of the seventeenth century which gave the opportunity for ' peaceful penetration ' by foreign musicians."

Mr. Riley's view is so thoroughly well accepted by nine out of ten general readers that his statement of it will probably pass half unnoticed by many of them. They are used to statements of this kind in the English history books from Macaulay onwards, and if corroboration were required they would easily find it in a dozen histories of music. One of the recent histories of music in England is that of Mr. Ernest Ford, and there they might find :—

" With the Commonwealth the voice of music was altogether silenced.

It needs no keen discernment to see the infinite possibilities of harm to the musical instincts of the country such a state of things opens out.

Imagine the thousands or millions of children born and brought up bereft of the happiness that music might have brought them.

We are told by the biologist that the continued disuse of muscles first renders them ineffective, and eventually leads to their extinction.

Similarly, completely separated from music as many were, they first became indifferent to it, and eventually lost all ear for it."

Now, it is very rude to say such a thing, but statements like those quoted show abysmal ignorance on the part of those who make them. Perhaps, however, it is not so much ignorance as want of thought. If Mr. Riley and Mr. Ford stopped for a moment to draw upon their knowledge of a few typical Puritans, they would eat their pens and drink their ink rather than employ them in disseminating such scandalous falsehoods.

Let us pick three typical Puritans. Can we do better than bring Cromwell, Milton, and Bunyan into the witness-box? Let us take Cromwell first.

The first regular State concerts began under Cromwell. Cromwell employed a private musician, John Hingston, who taught his daughters music, and, with two boy pupils, was in the habit of singing to his master the Latin motets of Richard Deering, "which Oliver was most taken with." Cromwell had an organ at Hampton Court Palace and another at Whitehall. Cromwell's Council of State nominated a committee to confer about the establishment of a " Corporation or College '" of music, and if the project never got beyond the stage of conferring and reporting, that is only what happens sometimes with Commissions to-day.

Milton was the son of a musician, and nobody who has read a few pages of his poems needs to be reminded how much he loved the art. In his tractate on education he lays it down that music should have a great place in training the young —following Plato closely in this respect.

As for Bunyan, they say that when he was a prisoner in Bedford Gaol he recreated himself by playing upon a flute of his own making, and surely *The Pilgrim's Progress* is full enough of music for anyone. " Then Christian gave three leaps for joy, and went on singing," says the Dreamer. That was when his burden rolled away; ever after he remained a singer, and at last entered the Celestial City to "melodious noise, in notes on high." When Christiana travelled she found at the Interpreter's House that "the Interpreter did usually entertain those that lodged with him with music at meals; so the minstrels played." Christiana "if need was could play upon the viol, and her daughter Mercy upon the lute," and once by the roadside "she played them a lesson and Ready-to-Halt would dance. So he took Despondency's daughter, named Much-Afraid, by the hand, and to dancing they went in the road. True he could not dance without one crutch in his hand; but I promise you he footed it well: also the girl was to be commended, for she answered the music handsomely."

The Puritans haters of music? Not a bit of it! Why, there was opera in London during the Puritan control, daily opera a part of the time. Read the list of music-books good John Playford issued; music-books poured from the press during the Commonwealth and Protectorate.

How, then, do these slanders against the Puritans originate? Probably in the fact that the Puritans did not like music in church. It is as though some historian of the future were to state "the English of the twentieth century hated novels," and, asked for his reasons, were to reply: "They never read them in church."

As for Mr. Athelstan Riley's idea that the period

of Puritan power brought English music to an end, let him be reminded that the greatest English musician came not before but *after the Commonwealth*—Henry Purcell.

IX

I.—AS IT WAS

WHEN young John Alden went on that love errand through the New England woods, for his friend Miles Standish, he came at length upon Priscilla spinning in her cottage.

> Open wide on her lap lay the well-worn psalm book of Ainsworth,
> Printed in Amsterdam, the words and music together,
> Rough hewn angular notes, like stones in the wall of a churchyard,
> Darkened and overhung by the running vine of the verses.
> Such was the book from whose pages she sang the old Puritan anthem.
>
> (Longfellow: *The Courtship of Miles Standish*).

Rarely nowadays may one see a copy of the " psalm book of Ainsworth," the great Hebraist who, exiled in Holland, " worked for some time as a porter in a booksellers," and " lived upon ninepence in the week with roots boyled." A monumental piece of work is that Puritan pastor's psalter, with its double version of all the psalms (prose and metre), with its learned annotations, and its solemn and sensible Preface.

31

" Tunes for the Psalms I find none set of God; so that each people is to use the most grave, decent and comfortable manner that they know how, according to the general rule."

The " most grave, comfortable and decent " that Ainsworth " knew how " were—

" most taken from our Englished psalms when they will fit the measure of the verse; and for the other long verses I have also taken (for the most part) the gravest and easiest tunes of the French and Dutch psalms."

Just the airs of the tunes he gave, in lozenge-shaped notes, without bars, " Rough-hewn, angular notes, like stones in the walls of a church-yard," as Longfellow calls them.

Probably the Mayflower pilgrims and the others who followed them to the Plymouth and Massachussets Bay colonies brought many copies not only of Ainsworth but also of Ravenscroft and of Sternhold and Hopkins. The Liturgy and its elaborate music for clergy and for choir they abhorred, but the simple psalm settings of the Church of England they had forsaken had no taint of prelacy, being the common property of non-Catholic Englishmen.

By and bye New England longed for a Psalm Book of its very own, and so, in 1640, on a press given by Puritan friends in Holland and set up in the house of the President of Harvard College, was printed " The New England Psalm Book," generally spoken of to-day as "The Bay Psalm Book." Crude as it was it went through 70 editions (some in England and Scotland) and did not fall entirely out of use until nearly 1800, though in many places the more polished "Tate and Brady" displaced it. The "Bay Psalm Book" is generally spoken of as the first printed book that the North American colonies ever produced.

Very curious was one attempt to supply something better than the famous "Bay" book. The great Cotton Mather, in 1718, was its author, and a special feature was the use of two kinds of type and of brackets, so that either long or short metre tunes could be used! There are some inventions too ingenious for the service of mortal man, and I fear that poor Cotton Mather never saw his Puritan friends flocking in their thousands to buy his work. Yet they needed some help, as witness this extract from the chronicle of a precentor, Judge Samuel Sewell (he made the entry in the very year that Cotton's adaptable psalter appeared).

"*Lord's Day, February 23rd,* 1718. I set York tune, and the congregation went out into St. David's in the very second going over. They did the same three weeks before. This is the second sign. I think they began in the last line of the first going over. This seems to me an intimation and call for me to resign the precentor's place to a better voice."

This was by no means the first trouble of the sort the good Judge had experienced. Thirteen

D

years earlier he had recorded how, after Mr. Pemberton had prayed " excellently," and Mr. Willard had preached " very excellently," it fell to him to set the tune, and he did so with no sort of excellence whatsoever.

" I intended Windsor and fell into High Dutch, and then, essaying to set another tune, went into a key much too high. So I prayed Mr. White to set it : which he did well, Litch-field tune. The Lord humble and instruct me, that I should be the occasion of any interruption in the worship of God."

Progress was ever a Yankee watchword, and it was not to be expected that the low state of musical cultivation implied by Judge Sewell's dis asters should last for ever. Singing Schools came into existence, choirs were common, the glories of four-part performance arose. Hymns (as distinct from metrical psalms) were introduced.

And with the opportunity the man—none other than William Billings, of Boston, tanner and tune-maker. Sang Billings—

" O praise the Lord with one consent,
And in this grand design
Let Britain and the Colonies
Unanimously join.'²

This was in 1770 : a few years later and Billings' tunes were being sung by Washington's army. No more " unanimously joining " of " Britain and the Colonies " for Billings and his New England brethren now! The first shot at Lexington put an end to all that.

What was Billings' speciality? Nothing less than the " fugue "²! Says he—

> " It has twenty times the power of the old slow tunes, each part straining for mastery and victory, the audience entertained and delighted, their minds surpassingly agitated and extremely fluctuated, sometimes declaring for one part, sometimes for another. Now the solemn bass demands their attention, next the manly tenor: now the lofty counter, now the volatile treble. Now here, now there: now here again—O ecstatic! Rush on, ye sons of harmony!"

Mastery, victory, entertainment, delight, agitation, " fluctuation," volatility, ecstasy—yes, but, William, where is the old Puritan *devotion?* Not in the congregation " sometimes declaring for one part, sometimes for another "; not in the choir, with its " volatile " treble, its " lofty counter," and its " manly tenor." Stay! there is the " solemn bass." Thank God there is *some* solemnity about the proceedings. The basses must surely have laid themselves open to the charge of " wet blanket "; never mind, basses! yours it is to maintain a little of the old dignity and composure that good Judge Sewell so much sorrowed to disturb. He would commend you. Perhaps, too, he would praise even more strongly a minister who was moved at that time to preach upon this text from the prophet Amos—*The songs of the temple shall be turned into howling.*

Many a book did the worthy fugue-loving tanner put into the hands of his fellow New Englanders. "American Choristers," "Singing Master's Assistants," "Psalm Singers' Amusements," and the like.*

Truth to tell, Puritan New England was more enterprising in these matters than New York and the other settlements, Anglican though they might be, and hence, as one would have imagined, in the tradition of English Church Music. Trinity Church, New York, secured an organ in 1741, and installed a choir of charity children, who sang by rote a few Tate and Brady psalms and a very simple anthem or two. New York was, in fact, awaiting *its* Billings. Happily he arrived in the

---

* " Fuguing tunes " were of course popular in England also at this period, and in the North they continued to enjoy a considerable measure of popularity almost to the present day, particularly with Nonconformist congregations. I possess a copy of the Halifax, 1811, edition of Chetham's *Psalmody* to which some owner has prefixed a sort of " black list " of " Objectionable Tunes." *Cranbrook* is one of these. It is a good sample of the class and has been reprinted so recently as 1904 in the Appendix to *The Methodist Hymn Book with Tunes.* South country and Anglican readers may care to see a bar or two.

person of William Tuckey, " Professor of the Theory and Practise of Vocal Music, late Vicar Choral of the Cathedral Church of .Bristol, and Clerk of the Parish of St. Mary Port in said city." As a publisher he became almost as prolific as Billings, and as parish clerk at Trinity Church he brought about, in 1769, the first performance of a *Te Deum* in the country. This is how he an-nounced it in the papers.

" To all lovers of Divine Harmony. Where-as it is the custom in Protestant congregations in Europe on times of rejoicing, as well as on an-nual or particular days of Thanksgiving, to sing the *Te Deum*, therefore, by particular desire, a subscription is opened for the encouragement of so laudable a practice in this city. Proposals as follows: Every lady, gentleman, etc., to sub-scribe whatever they please, for which subscrip-tion money William Tuckey has obligated him-self to teach a sufficient number of persons to perform the Te Deum, either with or without an organ or other instruments, and that it shall be as good a piece of music as any of the common *Te Deums* sung in any Cathedral in England."

II.—AS IT IS

WHAT of Church Music to-day in America? Are its ideals worthy? Is its practice pure? These are questions I can only answer tentatively. I have attended services in Anglican, Methodist, and Presbyterian Churches in New York, Boston, and elsewhere, have had many talks with church musicians, and have diligently studied the press, musical and general. This is, however, a very insufficient preparation for the answering of questions so momentous as those I have posed. The only thing seems to be to give my opinions frankly and to trust that they may possess a certain value.

First let us look at the evidence of the press. Here are some announcements from the advertisement or news columns of American papers :—

From New York papers—

THE NEW THOUGHT CHURCH, Aeolian Hall, 32 to 36, West 43rd Street. Sundays, 11 a.m. *F. W. Sears, M.P. Speaker. Finest Pipe Organ in the World, Youngest Organist in the World.*

At Calvary Episcopal Church, to-morrow night, the " Service of Lights," which has been held in Calvary parish for the last three years on Quinquagesima Sunday, will take place. This is a unique service, in that the worshipper is led to review the life of Christ through the reading of the Scripture, the music of the choir, and the lighting of the church. The choir enters a brilliantly illuminated church. As the Christmas music begins, a star high in the dome over the choir blazes out, announcing the birth of the Saviour. Then, as the service progresses, the reading of the lessons, the sombre tone of the music, and the slowly darkening church, portray to the mind that the life work of the Master is soon to end. When Calvary is reached, the church is in total darkness, save for the candle light; the music is characteristic of the passion, and in place of the star the cross is seen. The choir goes out in solemn procession, each one carrying a lighted candle. After they have left the church, the solo boy, standing in a gleam of light, sings "The Strife is O'er." The choir will be augmented by an orchestra of trumpets and drums. There will be an organ recital at 7-30, Mrs. Edwards assisting with a violin.

POPULAR VESPERS, CHAPEL OF THE INTERCESSION, Broadway and 155th Street—4 p.m., Thomas Farmer, jr., Baritone, will sing Confutatis, from Verdi's "Requiem." Leo Riggs, Recital Organist, will play the Prelude and Chorus from "Lohengrin." Dr. Gates will read selections from the Epistle to Timothy.

The Rev. W. John Murray, pastor of the Church of the Healing Christ, holding services in the laurel room of the Hotel Astor, has returned and will speak to-morrow morning on "God is Omnipresent." The musical programme will be : Last Hope, Gottschalk; Prelude in C♯ minor, Rachmaninoff; piano, Rafael Samuell; Abendlied, Schumann; Kol Nidrei, Bruch; violin, Henry Liff; vocal (selected), Mrs. Marie Donavin, Sondheim; Träumerei, Schumann; Finale, Chopin.

From a Pittsburgh paper—

The regular month-end musical service which has been maintained at the Point Breeze Presbyterian Church for the past four years, has been changed to the first Sunday in the month, and the new series

will be inaugurated to-night with the following programme, under the direction of E. Ellsworth Giles : —

Quartet—" I have Longed for Thy Salvation " (from *Stabat
   Mater*)   ...   . Rossini
Trio—" Father, Lead Me " (from *Belshazzar*)   Butterfield
Baritone Solo—" It is Enough " (from *Elijah*) Mendelssohn
Quartet—" Sun of My Soul " (from *Lohengrin*) ... Wagner
Quartet—" Crossing the Bar "   ...   . Nevin
Quartet—" Along the River of Time "   ...   ... Root

Probably most British readers will agree that
there is in each of these announcements the evidence of a wrong attitude towards music. In most
cases the emphasis seems to be misplaced. The
whole style of these announcements in certain
cases, implies that music is considered *an attraction.* " Leo Riggs, recital organist, will play the
Prelude and Chorus from *Lohengrin,*" consorts
badly with its accompanying statement, " Dr.
Gates will read selections from the Epistle to
Timothy." One wonders what Timothy himself
would think of it! Gottschalk, Rachmaninoff, and
Chopin seem hardly in place in " the Church of
the Healing Christ." " Finest Pipe Organ in the
World; Youngest Organist in the World," seems
an incongruous juxtaposition in any case, and it
appears as though " New Thought " in itself were
but a feeble attraction to the public of New York.
The " Service of Light " at Calvary Episcopal
Church strikes the sober matter-of-fact Briton as a
trifle theatrical. The Point Breeze Presbyterian
Church at Pittsburgh cannot be congratulated on
any vigour or masculinity in its programme for

the monthly musical service, and one wonders what the quartet, *Sun of my Soul,* from *Lohengrin,* may be.

There is, I think, undoubtedly a weakness exposed here. These announcements may not be quite typical (I hope they are not). Yet the American church-going public does to a large extent put music in too prominent a place; instead of making music " the handmaid of religion," it makes religion an excuse for music.

SPECIAL MUSICAL SERVICES

Take some further evidence. In the " New York Evening Post " of February 13, 1915, I find particulars of fifteen special musical services. The music announced is as follows :—

Dubois	-	*Seven Last Words.*
Gaul	- -	*Holy City* (in three churches).
,,	- -	*Ruth.*
Goss	- -	*The Wilderness.*
Gounod	-	*Gallia* (in three churches).
,,	-	*Babylon's Wave.*
,,	-	*Day of Penitence.*
Maunder	-	*Olivet to Calvary.*
Mendelssohn		*Hymn of Praise.*
Rossini	-	*Stabat Mater.*
Stainer	-	*Crucifixion.*

On the whole, not a *strong* list. Masculinity
again missing. Here are pretty tunes and emotional effect, but not a great deal of dignity. The
atmosphere does not seem quite healthy, somehow.
Query: can a virile religious life thrive in it?
There is a large preponderance of the modern
French and Italian schools, and of English music
that probably largely derives from these schools.

Again, I do not know that this is typical. I
can only say that, in fairness, I have not picked,
but have reprinted the whole list included in a
newspaper taken at random.

Now take, from the same source, a day's ordinary service list. Here I have confined myself
to the Anglican Churches of the city, and, for
purposes of comparison, have given later a list
of London Church music on the same Sunday,
The Times being my authority.

" SERVICE " MUSIC IN NEW YORK CHURCHES

Alcock in B♭ (M.).
Clark, Benedicite in E♭.
Cruichshank in G (E.).
Donizetti in C.
Dykes in F (M.).
Field in D (E).
Frost, Benedicite in D.
Gadsby in C (E.).
Garrett in D (E.).
Gounod, Mass of the Sacred Heart.

Hawley in E♭ (M. and E.).
Jackson, Te Deum in F.
King Hall in B♭ (M. and E.),
King Hall, Communion in C.
Lutkin in C (M.).
Martin in B♭ (E.).
Noble in B minor (M).
Parker in E (three churches) (M.).
Schilling in C (M).
Stainer, Te Deum and Benedicite in A and D.
Stainer in E♭ (two churches) (M.).
Stanford in B♭ (three churches) (M.).
Tours, Communion in C.
Whiting, Benedicite in D.
Whiting, Te Deum and Jubilate in A.
Wood in F (E.).

ANTHEMS

Bortniansky	*Cherubim Song (a cappella).*
Brahms	*Blest are they that mourn.*
Calkin	*Behold, now praise the Lord.*
Cobb	*O put your trust.*
Dvorák	*Eia Mater (Stabat Mater).*
Elgar	*Jesu, Word of God.*
Foster (Myles B.)	*O for a closer walk (two churches).*
Gounod	*Happy are we.*
,,	*Zion's ways do languish.*
Heinrich	*Hear us, O Father.*
Hills	*Wherewithal shall a young man?*

Hollins	· ·	*Rejoice in the Lord.*
Martin	· ·	*Whoso dwelleth.*
,,	· ·	*Hear my Prayer.*
,,	· ·	*Hail, gladdening Light.*
Mendelssohn	·	*Hear ye, Israel.*
,,	·	*He watching over Israel.*
,,	·	*The Sorrows of Death.*
Noble	· ·	*Come, O thou Traveller.*
Spicker	· ·	*Why art thou cast down?*
Stainer	· ·	*Lead, kindly Light.*
Sullivan	· ·	*I will mention.*
Sydenham	· ·	*Be merciful to me.*
Rossini	· ·	*Inflammatus.*
Thorne	· ·	*It is the Lord's mercies.*

Undoubtedly this is better—far better. What strikes one, of course, is the *complete* absence of anything of the English 16th, 17th, or 18th century schools, and this confirms what I have long suspected—that for the American church musician the English school begins with Stainer, Barnby and Sullivan. Is this so? Perhaps some American reader will enlighten me. If I am right there is another weakness exposed, and surely not unconnected with the one previously pointed out: probably it is the impersonality and seriousness of the earlier English composers, as much as their earlier idiom, that has delayed their appreciation. I have heard Gibbons in F sung, it is true, but it was given (as sometimes it is in this country) in a rather lifeless way, and a heavy organ accompaniment was maintained throughout. There are lots of Church music reformers in America, and one must hope that they will feel called upon ere long to carry through a propaganda for the more frequent and more understanding performance of that school of English church music that is one of the greatest glories of Protestantism. Such a propaganda is needed in England also.

" SERVICE " MUSIC IN LONDON CHURCHES

Calkin in B♮ (M.).
Cooke in G (E.).
Davies in G (M. and E.).
Dykes in F (M.).
Garrett in D (M).
   „   in E (E.).
Harwood in A♮ (M.) (three churches).
   „   in A♮ (E.).
Lloyd in E♮ (M.) (two churches).
Macpherson in E♮ (Communion).
Martin in G (E.).
Mendelssohn (Communion).
Schubert in B♮ (Communion).
Stainer in B♮ (M.).
Stanford in A (Communion).
Sullivan in D (M.).
Tomblin in C (E.).
Turle in D (E.).
Walmisley in D (E).
Wesley in E (Communion).

ANTHEMS AND INTROITS

Bach	*O Fount of Love.*
Battishill	*Behold how good.*
Boyce	*I have surely found.*
Cornelius	*Love, I give myself.*
Dering	*Jesu, the very thought.*
Garrett	*Our Soul on God.*
Leslie	*Love, holy, Christian pure.*
Mendelssohn	*Hear my Prayer.*
,,	*Lift thine eyes.*
	They that in much tribulation.
,,	*If with all your hearts.*
Oakeley	*Comes at times.*
Pergolesi	*O Lord, have mercy.*
Schubert	*Where Thou reignest* (two churches).
Wesley	*Blessed be the God* (six churches).

X

THE American is not above telling a story against himself. Here is one he tells.

A Harvard youth came bounding out of the examination room after a Divinity paper and burst into a group of his classmates with—

" Say, fellows, who *is* this Jehovah they are asking us so much about ? "

Now it happens that it was the Dean of the Faculty of Theology at Harvard who entertained me most hospitably when I visited that University. Perhaps I am on that account biassed, but—I do not believe the story.

Nevertheless it serves the purpose of reminding one of a common British charge against American education—that of superficiality. This charge occurs sometimes in the Report of the Moseley Commission, which in 1903 went out from England to investigate and report on American educational methods and results. For instance, Mr. W. C. Fletcher (now Chief Inspector of Secondary Education), speaking of the schools, said, "The quality of the work is distinctly mediocre. In some respects, probably, the average work is better than ours, but I saw little or none that an English

47

examiner or inspector would call good." That
was twelve years ago; progress has probably been
made, and anyone who has seen the improvements
of which our own Secondary Education during the
period since then has been capable will admit that
the statement may no longer be so true. I am
inclined to think, however, that, as regards music,
at any rate (in both schools and colleges) there
is still *something* in it. Yet, as I shall show, the
fact is far from altogether discreditable when its
cause is understood.

I think I should explain it in this way. The
Americans *love Education* in a way the Englishman hardly realises. Education is, with them, not
something thrust upon them by their Government,
but something for which they actually cry out.
That is one point. The next is that the Americans
are a very *enterprising* people. Now that exploration is exhausted and the whole land more or less
settled, they have turned commerce into a romance and education into an adventure. Then,
finally, they are wonderful *organisers*. See their
bad streets—surely the worst in the world—and
you would say the last thing they could do would
be to organise a city. Yet their very bad streets
are the result of most perfect organisation; political
parties, and " rings," and grafters of all kinds
have organised so wonderfully that they have, for
the time, been able to chain up one of the strongest
of American forces—civic pride. In New York,
Tammany has been made into so powerful a sys-
tem that for over a century it has largely controlled

the municipality. Here one organisation has throttled another.

Take these three qualities together (love of education, enterprise and organising ability) and see how they affect music in education. The American really believes in education, and he begins to realise that the arts have an enormous part to play in education—music, perhaps, especially. Immediately he says, " Let us, then, have music! " Then, since he has a courageous enterprise, he is not at all the man to say, " What are the accredited systems of musical education amongst the older civilisations?" He looks at the matter for himself, looks at it with a " fresh eye "; goes to the heart of the question, gets a big conception, and is not afraid of it when he has got it. That done, he brings a vast organisation into existence, and does so with a burst of energy that leaves no time for the steady growth of a large class of good men trained to handle it.

If, then, the American musician is sometimes found to be behind his British brother in downright detailed thoroughness it is because he is before him in energy and invention. In some cases he is doing on a large scale work at which we are only just beginning cautiously to nibble. He must make some mistakes because he is doing a new thing, and if we are wise we shall not smile at his mistakes but profit by them. His experiments we ought to watch with the greatest interest, for from them we may learn: where he leads we may some day want to follow.

Take, as the most obvious instance, the "appreciative" teaching of music. Brave men in England have put up a fight for this. Gradually it is winning its way into secondary schools of the best class (more particularly girls' schools at present). Largely it is the music teachers themselves (all honour to them!) who have grasped the importance of this side of musical education and are pressing it upon the attention of headmasters and headmistresses and education authorities. As yet, however, we have few teachers qualified to teach the subject intelligently, and the progress of its recognition, though steady, is slow. In America, on the other hand, Musical Appreciation appears to be a recognised subject in most colleges and universities. The authorities prescribe it and the professors have it to teach. In some you may take it as a subject for entrance (our "Responsions," "Previous," or "Matriculation"); in most you may take it as a part of the degree work. The thing has been organised right away, and without waiting to train teachers of the subject. The American when he gets a good idea does not wait to talk about it; he puts it into execution!

And so, in a Women's College, I heard a most admirable lecture (or rather conversation, for the students themselves were freely drawn upon for ideas) on one of Beethoven's Sonatas. The class was going through the whole of the thirty-two, as work for two terms, and in the third term would take, similarly, two of Wagner's Music Dramas.

So far as I could gather these masterpieces were being treated in much the same way as the plays of Shakespeare or the poems of Browning might be treated in a course on English literature. Superficial the work might be called, and probably a good many of the students would justify this view by their answers if you came to question them minutely on the music they had been studying. But then this is comparatively new work, either in America or Britain; it has been going on in those countries only a few years, and France and Germany, so far as I know, have not yet started it. Wait a few years longer and the experience of the American professors who are teaching the subject will be pooled for the benefit of all concerned; books upon it will be multiplied, and then gradually the treatment will be tightened up until the charge of superficiality can no longer be made.

XI

CHRISTMAS EVE MUSIC IN A NEW YORK SQUARE
A WAR-TIME CELEBRATION

" SKY-SCRAPER Square " it might well be called for the buildings around its modest plot of grass have heavenward aspirations. Please don't imagine that height means ugliness. Look around to-night and see the famous " flat-iron " building at one corner, scintillating brightness from each of its thousand windows, or the still more famous Metropolitan Life Building, at the next corner, glistening white throughout an expanse of wall and window sufficient for a good-sized town—see these and their many brother giants, drawn up like an army of protection around the crowd of pigmy humans gathered on the gravel walks, and admit that the Sky-scraper has its own poetic glory.

From the fifty-storey tower of the Metropolitan floats down the chime of bells, announcing the ceremonies that are to follow. As the bells at last lapse into silence the trumpeters on the temporary staging in the middle of the Square come forward and blow a vigorous fanfare. Three times do they blow it, and then from the Church to the East (once so bold but now reduced to tiny insignificance, wedged in among sky-scrapers eight or ten times its height) come the strains of *Adeste Fideles*.

Led by a band of brass, and strongly guarded by the ubiquitous boy scout, there files into the Square a choir of men and women who have volunteered for this public service. Twice through the finest of all Christmas hymns is sung, before they all are gathered on the platform under the many-coloured electric illuminations of its awning.

Now, as the choir continues singing, all eyes are turned to the noble Christmas tree which has been placed in the centre of the Square. Suddenly the Star of Bethlehem, which crowns it, bursts into white light, and then, one by one, the many branches glow with red and blue, green and golden yellow until at last the whole tree is resplendent with tiny electric bulbs.

Then more Carols—beautiful old *Heilige Nacht* from Germany; *The First Nowell* and *Good King Wenceslas* from England. Oh! the irony of this mingling of the warring nationalities in the songs of Peace and Goodwill! But New York is the most cosmopolitan city in the world, and evidences of this are everywhere. See such now as Os-Ke-Non-Ton, a Mohawk Indian in all the glory of his feathers, leads the singing of a hymn written for this very evening by a New York clergyman of Portugese name and origin, to the tune of our British National Anthem.*

---

* The papers of words which have been distributed and the lantern sheet exhibited call the air *My country, 'tis of Thee;* but the Americans are not the only people who think of our National Anthem as their own.

" May earth no more rehearse
War's songs of crime and curse,
O, make War cease!"

sing the crowd in the Square, and as they do so
there is a pop, a flash and a puff, as a press
photographer secures the picture of us he wants
for to-morrow morning's paper. A pop, a flash
and a puff—away over the seas, half Europe sees
and hears these multiplied and magnified by many
thousands, and the crowd puts feeling into the
singing of the next lines.

" Death tube and shrieking shell
Sound for brave men the knell,
Widows the chorus swell—
God send us peace!"

The chimes in the fifty-storey tower tell us that
it is six o'clock, and the celebration is over. Call
not America hard, business-mad, and hustling!
Think of the poetry and the religious feeling that
have found their expression in this public recognition of the place that Christianity still holds in
the hearts of men. And be sure that, as the chimes
die away, there are some in the crowd whose
thoughts turn to Bruges and Malines and other
cities far across the Atlantic, whose carillon towers
have been long silent. Some there must be
amongst the throng who mutter a prayer for the
speedy coming of the day when from those towers
shall peal forth the happy tones that tell of the
last enemy expelled.

XII

A COLONY FOR CREATIVE WORKERS

THE artist, be he musician, painter, or poet, who can do fine creative work amid the smoke and dust, the din and clatter of a busy town, must indeed be independent of his environment. A few artists of this hardy temperament do exist, a small and select number who can breathe in the air of the city and delight in it; who find their inspiration in the ceaseless movement of the life around them. But for the majority, the busy town which offers the only chance of artistic study and environment, binds and clogs the creative impulse.

It was this fact Edward MacDowell realised, and it led him in the last years of his life to express a wish that there were some place where all artists could find inspiration; where every sense should be stimulated by the beauty of the surroundings, and where activity of brain should not be gained at the expense of bodily health.

Some years before, MacDowell had built for himself a log cabin in a lonely and beautiful spot on the New Hampshire Hills. Here he used to retire to work in the summer, and it was here, after his death, that Mrs. MacDowell resolved to plant the foundation stone of the colony now

spoken of as the " American Mecca for Artists,"
thus carrying out her husband's great wish. She
was aided in her task by the Mendelssohn Club
of New York, whose conductor MacDowell had
been for many years. The Club formed a Mac-
Dowell Memorial Association, whose object should
be to realise, as far as possible, the Composer's
last desire, and from this has arisen a colony which
bids fair in time to be " one of the great art cen-
tres of the world."

And now let us take a peep at this colony at
work and see how the workers spend their days.

" The first rule of the colony is absolute personal liberty, therefore each may see as little
or as much of his fellow workers as he desires.
One may practically live alone in this place of
harmony and cause no comment, for all work
towards success and find no time for the ordinary
small talk of the average school."

So comments Miss Alice Chapman in an Article
in *The Opera Magazine* (New York). She continues :—

" The order of the day is breakfast at seven-
thirty, after which all go to their work, either
in the studios or the open woods, taking their
luncheon with them, although sometimes it is
sent to them at the studios, if their work is
confining. . . . . Dinner is served at six-thirty,
after which the workers are free to follow their

own desires for work or play as inclination
prompts. Abundant vegetables are raised on the
farm for the tables, and the students reap the
benefits of the economic mind of Marian Mac-
Dowell in this as in other respects, for it is to
her that they owe the luxuries they enjoy. Nothing goes to waste at Hillcrest; even the small
plots of ground must do their share in helping
the cause along by producing the vegetables.

"In the deep woods not far from the 'Holy
of Holies' Cabin* the community has cleared
a broad woodland stage—100 by 125 feet, with
a wonderful background of pines, whose trunks
help to carry out the illusion that many people
are frolicking here and there among the old
trees as the lights flicker through them, while
old Monadnock rises in all its grandeur as a
fitting setting for this odd stage. Here every
year in the month of August a festival or pageant
is held, lasting an entire week, the fame of
which is becoming almost as far-reaching as that
of Bayreuth and Oberammergau. . . . Mrs. Mac-
Dowell is the wheel round which everything re-
volves; her energy is unbounded, and the
students as well as farm folk, adore her. Six
months of the year she gives every moment of
her waking hours to the work, as well as most
of her income, and to-day knows more than most
men about road-building, model dairies, stone
walls, carpentering, painting and house-building.
. . . . The visitor will meet her at every turn,

* MacDowell's Log Cabin.

interviewing workmen, inspecting their work, marking out new roads, or selecting some secluded spot for a new studio; her cheery smile continually brightening the world around her."

And with this glimpse of Mrs. MacDowell employing all her energies and talents in this great work, we must take leave of the colony, carrying back to town with us a memory of mountains and forests, of a community of free and happy beings working out their artistic ideals each in their individual way; and with what results? Perhaps the music of the future generation will hold the answer to that question.

XIII

THE HOME OF A GREAT QUARTET

A BEAUTIFUL house on Eighty-fifth Street, New
York. Everywhere busts or portraits of musicians
and engravings of musical subjects—in the hall,
on the walls of the staircase; at the head of the
stairs the host and hostess receiving their guests
Pass on, after their word of greeting, into the
large room where a number of the friends of the
house are already assembled, standing in chatting
groups or seated informally here and there about
the room. By and bye the host strolls in, and
four members of the throng emerge from its mass,
reach their instruments, and step on to the platform. The music begins.

It is a new work, to us at any rate, and, so
far as we can find, to all there—a Quartet by one
Bernstein, rather difficult to enjoy completely on
a first hearing, probably a little dry even on a
second or third, but with a brilliant Scherzo. When
it is over the guests fall a-talking and discuss the
music. Then the host walks across to a cabinet
and takes out a set of parts. Here is a Haydn
Quartet, something every listener can enjoy, and
given in a way that shows the players love it too.

59

> " . . . Lo, Haydn at the door
> Enters like some stiff angel from his frame, . .
> Bearing the bundle of his latest score
>   Which he distributes, smiling, to the blessed four.
>   But is not Haydn dead? He dies no more
> So long as these shall meet! The magic wand
> Brings the old master through the shadowy door,
> And upright in the midst his soul doth stand
> While through the chords his sunny force doth pour
> —Ah, Haydn, hast thou truly ever lived before?"

This over, the sliding doors to the left fall apart and all flock through to the next room. The thirsty players solace themselves with beer, or claret, or tea, or coffee, or chocolate, the guests likewise; menservants and maidservants move about with trays of gaily coloured cakes, cigars are lighted, the host and hostess pass from group to group, with a word here and a word there; all around is a buzz of musical conversation, critical, reminiscent or humorous.

It is one of the Saturday afternoon meetings of the famous Flonzaley Quartet at the house of its founders, Mr. and Mrs. Edward J. de Coppet.

Why " Flonzaley," by the way? Well " flonz," in the patois of the Suisse Romande, means a stream; " aley " is a diminutive. Flonzaley, then, means " little stream," and from that natural feature an estate takes its name. It lies on the shore of Lake Geneva: here Mr. de Coppet (Swiss in origin) has his country house, and here, year by year, the Quartet's concert tours in America and Europe and its members' well-earned holidays in their various native countries concluded, Messrs.

Betti, Pochon, Ara and d'Archambeau gather to prepare once more, under the eye of their director, for a further season of strenuous, happy work for themselves and of pure, undiluted musical enjoyment for their large and widely spread public. The party might have been called the " de Coppet Quartet," but its founder has preferred to give it an impersonal title and to let it sail forth under the flag of its old world headquarters.

Twelve years ago the Quartet was born, but a full quarter century has passed since happy parties of friends first gathered at Mr. de Coppet's New York house to hear the music that was made there. The first violin in those early days was Charles Bouis, a gifted pupil of César Thomson and brother of Mrs. de Coppet (who from then to now has herself splendidly sustained the piano part in works that included such). The Quartet was then partly amateur in its constitution, and year by year its members met at the de Coppet house on St. Cecilia's Day and reviewed the musical doings of the past twelve months. The enthusiasm, the ripe judgment and the keen musical conscience of the master of the house held before them ideals of perfection and inspired them with the determination to strive after those ideals. A visit to New York of the Kneisel Quartet (now permanently established there) set a new standard and gave new vigour to the enterprise. When, on Mr. Bouis' departure for Europe, the present Flonzaley Quartet was founded, it succeeded to the Kneisel inspiration of its predecessors, and ever since the Kneisels and the Flonzaleys have worked in the friendliest and most helpful rivalry.

Recently some of Mr. de Coppet's friends celebrated the completion of the tenth year of life of the present Quartet by a supper and presentation, and the Toastmaster asked a riddle, " Why has New York probably the greatest two Quartets of the world?" The answer, at first hearing, is just as great a riddle—" Because it has them both!" The interpretation thereof the riddler thus expressed—" They learn from each other, they stimulate each other, and I do not believe that either of them would be the great quartet it is if they were not in constant association with each other. The most beautiful harmony that I know in music is the harmony between these two quartets."

The Kneisel Quartet, by the way, this year celebrates its 30th year of life, so it is, by a long stretch of time, the elder of the two.

At the festive occasion just alluded to, Mr. Ugo Ara, the gifted viola of the Quartet, harrowed the feelings of those present by this black picture of life in a quartet.

" Have you ever imagined the terrible slavery of these four ' Siamese Brothers ' condemned to play, to bow and to smile, to dine, to rehearse and . . . . to pose for the photographer all at the same time and in perfect tempo?

" Have you ever realised the crushing burden of this triple married life in which every one of us depends constantly and entirely on the good

will, the moods and the caprices of his better
.... ' *three quarters* ' ? ''

But a glance at the jovial faces of Mr. Ara and
his companions warns us not to take him too
seriously. To be truthful, they bear their " terrible
slavery " and " crushing burden " without appar-
ent utter exhaustion.

Many an anecdote has Mr. Ara of the experiences
of his colleagues and himself on their travels.
Here, in closing, are one or two of his tales.

" On one of our early tours we went to Amsterdam, where we had to play Hugo Wolf's beautiful
and difficult String Quartet. The first movement
went well. But in the beginning of the adagio,
where we had to play some very dangerous and
complicated chords, I noticed a man in the third
row making evident signs of disapprobation. Of
course it disturbed me terribly and I determined
not to look at him again. But involuntarily, every
time I had something difficult to play I looked at
my man, and noticed with terror that he was making the most awful faces. I was in despair, and
my colleagues too. But what was our surprise
when in the artist-room we found the man in
question asking us very kindly to put our signa-
tures in his album and assuring us that seldom
had he heard such a beautiful ensemble and never
in his life a quartet playing so perfectly (gr .... l),
but so perfectly (gr ....!), but so perfectly
(gr ....!) in time! The man had a nervous
tick—a wonder that we didn't get one too! ''

" In a small place near Boston, one evening

after the concert, we met at the station a lady who wanted to know all about our instruments—'What kind of instruments do you have?'—'Old Italian instruments.'—'Oh, I thought so.'—'And what about their makers?'—'Stradivari and Guadagnini.'—'Oh . . . . I thought so.—And what about their age?'—'Two hundred years old.'—'Oh . . . . I thought so.'

"'Madame,' we said to her, 'you seem to be quite a connoisseur.'—'Oh no,' she answered very modestly, 'I am not. But it is easy to see that you have very valuable instruments. It is extraordinary all I could hear in your playing! Sometimes human voices.—Sometimes bird songs.—And sometimes (and here her voice trembled with emotion) and sometimes even . . . . *dogs barking.*'"

"In a small place in the Middle West we were very much surprised, coming from the concert, to find the hotel-keeper, who had received us very cordially on our arrival, absolutely changed and directly angry with us. We couldn't understand the reason. But very soon he told us frankly: 'You boys had a fine business, but you put mine " on the blink." I run the moving-picture show in this town. Everybody went to your concert and I had an empty house.' And soon after, as though he had struck a glorious idea: 'Now, boys,' he said, 'Why can't we do business together? What about playing for me three shows a day—one hundred dollars a week?'

"We were foolish enough to decline it. Why!

to-day some nice little selections of .... Schönberg at the 'movies' would, perhaps, make quite a sensation!!"

"A lady, who had known the Quartet for years but had never heard it, told me she intended to come to our second concert at the Aeolian Hall. Knowing the lady is not very musical and that we were going to play the Schönberg, I said to her: ' Oh, please, Madam, don't come to *that* concert. We are going to have such an awful hard programme!' And she said to me very gently: ' Oh, it doesn't matter, Mr. Ara, it doesn't matter at all. I am not so critical!'"

Mr. de Coppet's death—a great loss to music—has occurred since the above was written. It is some comfort to hear that the work of the Quartet will be carried on just as before.

F

XIV

A " MUSIC SETTLEMENT "

DOWN the Bowery, with a shouting mob at his heels, ran Toney Palermo, an Italian labourer, firing a revolver as he ran. Two of the " Black Hand " were after him, he said, and they had given him the sign that means death.

In the streets that day there was excitement everywhere. Not content with the capture of Toney Palermo, for what the official language mildly described as " disorderly conduct," the detectives put into safe ward Vincenzo Proverzamo, for carrying a stiletto, an automatic pistol and a box of cartridges, and Giorlano Martorano, for being found in possession of a revolver.

That very afternoon I took my wife down the Bowery on a quiet little tour of exploration. There are more ways than one, of course, of spending a pleasant Sunday afternoon, and we neither took part in any revolver practice nor, as it happened, witnessed such. What we did see I will describe.

A crowd of young people are entering a small concert hall. Most of them are Jews, but a good many races are represented (including that of

Toney, who is disporting himself in the streets, and of Vincenzo and Giorlano, private proprietors of neighbouring arsenals). Some of these young people carry violin cases, others carry nothing beyond their best clothes and a happy smile. Before the door are three or four lordly automobiles with gaudy princes for chauffeurs—strange contrast between the squalid streets and the luxurious vehicles, between lowly Toney & Co., on the one hand, and their lofty high-and-mightinesses, the chauffeurs, on the other; between down-town poverty and up-town pride. What is it all about? Come inside and see!

Evidently this is a place of musical instruction. There are little rooms, each with its piano. There are big ones lined with books—every recent work upon music you can think of is there, and on the tables are the musical papers. In the centre of the building is the concert hall, fast filling with an audience. Kind officials, wishing to show favour to British musicians, give us seats near the front, and, as we take them, the sound of tuning in the next room ceases and a string orchestra breaks into the slow and solemn strains of an old chorale. A verse or two by a men's voice choir follows. This over, the players file into the concert hall and take their places at the music desks. The conductor turns to the audience and announces a piece of Svendsen. There are about thirty-five fiddlers, and their band is well balanced, well trained, and well conducted. Svendsen ended, Arensky is announced —Variations on a Theme of Tchaïkovsky, *Christ when a Child.* Here we get really good tone and fine playing.

Then the conductor turns to the audience and makes a little speech. This is a " Music Settlement," the New York Music Settlement, mother of smaller settlements in many cities of the Union. Its fifteen years' development is briefly sketched in the conductor's address. There are, he says, in the orchestra we have just heard, one or two who began their instruction fifteen years ago, when the Settlement opened; others are comparative newcomers. The whole idea of the Settlement is not to encourage concert playing but to foster *home music.* A strong *esprit de corps* is one of the prides of the institution. Some students have worked their way forward in the world of music and gone to Europe for study; they always come back to help, however. This afternoon's programme, we are told, is to be largely carried out by the younger students, and this announcement made, the director calls on a little girl for the first movement of a Haydn Piano Sonata.

How *do* they do it? These children have all the maturity of thoughtful adult artists. This girl, for instance, has real *style.* A little Russian Jew boy follows; he is about to play from the floor of the house, but is stopped in time and made to ascend the platform, an incident which awakens a boyish bashfulness. He plays one of the Kreisler arrangements, a *Prelude* and *Allegro* by Pugnani; his intonation is perfect and he displays a very clear *staccato.*

Next comes another orchestral piece, the Quintet from *The Mastersingers,* arranged. The volume of tone in this is a surprise. A little girl of about fourteen follows, playing two *Songs without Words,* and then a boy humorist of twelve or thirteen plays another Kreisler arrangement, a Minuet of Porpora, as only a born joker can. Then come two movements of Beethoven's pianoforte Trio in D♭. From a pedestal at a corner of the platform Beethoven looks on approvingly (not turning his back on the whole proceedings—as he does at our own Royal Philharmonic concerts!) So the programme proceeds. The wonder is that you listen to these children not because they *are* children, but because they are musicians. You think, all the time, " How well that is played! " and not " How wonderful *for such a child!*"

What is the idea of the whole thing? I find it best expressed in the following sentence from an article by Marian Claire Smith :—

> " In these later days we are realising that life is more than meat, to the toiling as well as to the leisured class, and that the right use of his imaginative faculties is quite as imperative a need of every child as food and clothing or the kind of training which shall enable him to secure these things for himself."

The Music School Settlement, Miss Smith continues, is " not a sentimental philanthropy." It has an intensely practical aim and is carried out in a very practical way.

What children are admitted to its benefits?

" From the child who seeks instruction here, but one qualification is required—an honest desire for it, and a readiness to make a sincere use of his chance. That he may or may not become so proficient as to make a professional musical career possible, is not the important consideration. That he shall have unlocked for him the Gates of Expression so that he may walk the sunlit paths of the Kingdom of the Ideal so far as his faltering steps can take him, is the work which seems to us worth while."

There is a little bit of American fine-phrasing about those last words. A sober British musician would be too self-conscious to talk about " Gates of Expression " and " Kingdoms of the Ideal," but the spirit of the thing is true and good.

———

Now for some facts about the New York Settlement. It has well over 1,000 pupils, representing 20 nationalities. The subjects taught include piano, violin, 'cello, double bass, voice, etc. There are Theory Classes, Sight-Singing Classes, five Orchestras and Ensemble Classes, and a Teachers' Class. The pupils pay for individual half-hour lessons, 25 cents. (1/-); for classes they pay 10 cents. (5d.). A limited number of scholarships provide for talented pupils who cannot pay fees.

There is a " Faculty " of 100, all but about ten of the teachers being paid, though not high fees. Each Department (Piano, Violin, Theory, etc.) is under the guidance of a Supervisor, and all are subject to the director (at the time of my visit Mr. David Mannes). In addition there are ten or twelve Residents, whose care is the social side of the work, though every teacher is supposed to be interested in this, too, for the whole outlook of the movement is a social one.

The balance sheet is interesting. Bear in mind the expense of New York life when you read that salaries to the teaching staff run away with £4,000, and to the Residents with nearly £700. The Director receives £750. As regards receipts, fees amount to about £2,000; an Endowment Fund provides about £800. Donations, etc., bring the total up to nearly £12,000.

The training of teachers is one of the cares of the Settlement. In America, as here, the music teaching in the poorer districts is abominable, and in helping teachers to qualify for better work the institution is widening its influence. In the Piano Department alone 100 normal students are at present at work.

The equipment of the Settlement is good. The library contains more than 7,000 pieces of music for free circulation, including all the miniature scores a reasonable person can desire. Other provision is in proportion.

The Symphony Orchestra does advanced work and gives concerts in various parts of the city to people who would otherwise rarely hear good music.

There is a Pianoforte Tuning Class for the Blind.

In summer a small camp in Newfoundland provides needed change for some of the children, and a day's outing in the country is provided for others. The "Playground Attendance" in July and August totals 12,500; the " Bath Attendance " 5,200.

Such are a few scattered facts about this, the premier Music School Settlement.   Those who wish for more should send a small sum to cover postage, etc., to its Secretary (at 55, East Third Street, New York), who would, I feel sure, be glad to send the Annual Report. Another useful publication is the Record of the Boston Music School Settlement (110, Salem Street, Boston, Mass.), and still another. is the Report of the National Association of Music School Societies (Elwood Hendrick, Secretary, 30, Pine Street, New York).

I should like to give a pretty full account of the Boston Settlement, for I have a note book with a lot of material collected from the mouth of its Associate Director, Daniel Bloomfield. But that must wait for another time, and for the moment I must content myself with a few extracts from its printed Report, which serve to illustrate Music School Settlement work in general.

"One of our teachers went to visit a pupil (teachers are required to visit their pupils) and was surprised to find that the address given was that of a barber shop. She entered the shop and there found Theresa practising on an old square piano while her father was attending to his customers.

" Gertrude, one of our old pupils, is now at Radcliffe,* and she finds time to practise the piano assiduously and to learn the mysteries of harmony and counterpoint. Lawrence, a pale-faced studious chap of sixteen, is now a freshman at Harvard, and is paying his way through the engineering course by playing the violin at a café in the evening. Isidore, with the help of his violin, is getting a medical education at Tufts. Several of our girls are at high school planning for a teacher's career. Jeanette, whose home has been on Hanover Street, had ambition enough to want to teach. She is now teaching in the North End schools and is helping the Settlement's children with their studies.

" The Settlement is cognizant of the disintegrating influences of the street, and it offers a wholesome substitute. I cannot repeat Nathan's case too often, for it indicates clearly to what extent the influence of the Music School Settlement can go. Nathan was brought before the Juvenile Court charged with a very serious offence—derailing a street car. The judge thought Nathan could make good if given a chance. Fortunately the probation officer knew that Nathan could play the violin a little. He was brought to the

* The Women's College of Harvard University.

Settlement and was invited to hear a children's ensemble group. It was the psychological moment for this boy. He became inspired with ambition to play. He was turned over to Miss Goodwin, who soon gained his confidence and who showed him what he could do if he tried. The result is a boy whose heart and soul are wrapped up in music, a boy who finds more pleasure in the intricacies of Bach than in the empty offerings of the street, and who has something for which to strive."

And thus, for this time, must end my account of Music Settlement work in America.

XV

CHRISTMAS MUSIC

Sir Roger de Coverley killed eight fat hogs at Christmas-time; he "dealt about his Chines very liberally amongst his Neighbours, and, in particular, he sent a string of Hogs-pudding with a pack of Cards to every poor Family in the Parish." "I have often thought," says Sir Roger, "it happens very well that Christmas should fall out in the middle of Winter. It is the most dead, uncomfortable Time of the Year, when the poor People would suffer very much from their Poverty and Cold if they had not good Cheer, warm Fires, and Christmas Gambols to support them." Hence the "Hogs-puddings" aforementioned; hence "a double Quantity of Malt to my small Beer" ("set a running for twelve Days to every one that calls for it"); hence the "Piece of cold Beef and a Mince-Pye" upon the table; and hence the "Plumb-porridge."

This is characteristic enough so far as it goes; eating and drinking were ever the Englishman's way of celebrating a domestic joy or a religious mystery. But what about the Christmas music? That we hear nothing of *that* is, we may be sure, not Sir Roger's fault, but that of his historian.

Surely the old mansion rang with song and dance, and the village fiddler and the wassailers were not the least important of the guests Sir Roger entertained with his doubly-malted small beer and his mince-pyes and plumb-porridge. Let us never doubt it, Sir Roger would see that the mirth of his fireside was not without its music.

How comes this connection of Christmas and song? Whence date our carols, and what is their origin? The learned in such matters refer us to the mystery plays of the Middle Ages, and ask us to hear in our Christmas music an echo of times long past, when Church and Stage, so far from being at enmity, were friends and colleagues.

———

It is Christmas Eve, and with the crowd of simple townsfolk we flock into the big church. There on the altar is a cradle, and beside it a figure of the Virgin Mother. By-and-by there is a stir at the west door, and flocking up the aisle come the shepherds, with crooks in their hands, and real sheep, with dogs to drive them. Some of the shepherds fall asleep; others watch their flocks. But a sudden blast from a trumpet rings out, and all start up with astonishment. Up in the pulpit is an angel, who proclaims the birth of the Christ. Then from the clerestory rings out the song of the " multitude of the heavenly host "— " Glory to God in the highest, and on earth Peace, Goodwill toward men." The shepherds crowd around the manger and adore the Child and His mother. Then round the church they go in procession, singing a hymn of joy and praise. Here, it is said (and in similar mysteries, acted all over the country), is the origin of our Christmas carol.

Here is a verse from a translation by Barnabe Googe which describes further some of the Christmas ceremonies and their music. I am indebted to Mr. Edmonstoune Duncan's *Story of the Carol* for calling my attention to it :—

" Three masses every priest doth sing upon that solemne day,
With offerings unto everyone, that so the more may play.
This done a wodden childe in clowtes is on the altar set,
About the which both boyes and gyrles do daunce and trymly
jet :
And carols sing in prayse of Christ, and, for to help them
heare,
The organs aunswer every verse with sweete and solemne
cheer.
The priests do rore aloude ; and round about their parentses
stand
To see the sport, and with their voyce do help them and
their hande."

Indeed the old Christmas folk-plays are full of music. The Coventry Nativity Play rings with the songs of the angels, the shepherds, and the gentle mothers in dread of Herod's men at arms. *Here the Angels sing " Gloria in Excelsis " again,* and *Here the Shepherds sing again,* are stage dircetions punctuating the play. Very happy is the shepherd's song :—

" As I rode out this enderes night,
Of three jolly shepherds I saw a sight,
And all about their fold a star shone bright ;
They sang, ' Terli, terlow ' ;
So merrily the shepherds their pipes can blow."

Quieter is that of the mothers :—

> " Lulla, lulla, thou little tiny child ;
>   By, by, lullay, lullay, thou little tiny child,
>   By, by, lullay, lullay."

When the shepherds come to the manger they offer the presents that loving simplicity suggests, one his hat, another his mittens, and the third his shepherd's pipe. The spirit of sacrifice is in each of the presents, and the offering of the pipe is symbolical and prophetic, for music has been the chief gift of Christian folk to the babe in the manger from that day to this.

Has not Cammaerts been misled in the matter of the gift of a shepherd's pipe, by the way? He has read this or some other old miracle play, and in his Noëls he has turned its quaint idea into one still quainter.

> " Le premier dit : ' Mon capouchon.'
>   Le deuxième dit : ' Mes gants de laine.'
>   Et le troisième : ' Ma pipe de porcelaine.'
>   Afin qu'il n'ait pas froid aux yeux.
>   Et qu'il ait bien chaud aux mains,
>   Et que, plus tard, au haut des cieux,
>   Il fume avec ses séraphins."

Devotion and humour were not so far apart in the fifteenth century as they are to-day. In the very choirs and chancels of their cathedrals and churches the architects could place grotesque carving, and in the Miracle Plays a touch of the comic is not lacking. The Wakefield Play has the boisterous fun of the blanket-tossing of a sheep-stealer, and perhaps there is intentional humour in the shepherds' approving criticism of the angels' song. Good musicians are the Yorkshire shepherds; earlier in the night they have shown themselves to be what Shakespeare's clown, in *A Winter's Tale*, describes as " three-men's song-men all," joining in a mirthful stave, one taking the " tenory," the other " the treble so high," and the third the " mean." Now, when the angel sings, like true choralist-critics, they fall to the technicalities of discussion :—

> " *First Shepherd:* ' *Say, what was his song?*
> *Heard ye not how he cracked it? Three breves*
> *to a long.*'
> *Second Shepherd:* ' *Yea, marry, he hacked it.*
> *Was no crotchet wrong, nor no thing that lacked it.*' "

The first printed collection of carols in this country was by Wynkyn de Worde, in 1521. No copy remains, alas! But in the Bodleian may be seen the end leaf, with the famous Boar's Head Carol (still to be heard each Christmas at Queen's College, Oxford), and as colophon, " Thus endeth the Christmasse caroles newly imprinted in London in Flete Strete at the signe of the Sonne."

Scotland lost her carols at the Reformation, England at the Commonwealth. The latter got hers back again; the former has never done so, nor, of course, did Christmas over the border ever again become a season of much account. The modern growth of interest in the old songs of Christmas, in the English Church, may perhaps be considered a by-product of the Oxford Movement. It has

even become a convention (an absurd one, perhaps) to imitate in the productions of to-day the
quaint verbal expressions and the modal pecu-
liarities of the music of pre-Reformation song. All
this is a little disquieting—as much as to say that
Christmas joy is an antiquarian revival rather than
a piece of real, present-day expression.

If, at Christmas, music is an offering of devotion
to the Deity, it is just as much an expression of
human happiness. Who could write a Christmas
story without bringing music into it? In Dickens
it is never lacking. Scrooge's *Ghost of Christmas
Past* shows him old Fezzywig's "fiddler with a
music book, who went up to the lofty desk and
made an orchestra of it and tuned like fifty
stomachaches." His *Ghost of Christmas Present*
whirled him through the air to where two light-
house-keepers " joined their horny hands over the
rough table and wished each other a Merry
Christmas in a can of grog. One of them—the
elder, too, with his face all damaged and scarred
with hard weather, as the figurehead of an old
ship might be—struck up a song that was like
a gale in itself." Then, away from the lighthouse,
Scrooge and the Ghost sped to sea, where on a
ship they "stood beside the helmsman at the
wheel, the look-out in the bow, the officers who
had the watch, dark ghostly figures in their several
stations, and every man amongst them hummed
a Christmas tune, or had a Christmas thought, or

spoke beneath his breath to his companion of some bygone Christmas Day, with home and thoughts belonging to it."

A few years ago since, in a certain ship's diary, one Captain Scott described another Christmas at sea. Of course a Christmas service comes into the story, with a " full attendance and a lusty singing of hymns." And, of course, again, there was a fine Christmas dinner—with " Penguin breast stewed as an entrée," and other good things either peculiar to the Antarctic or common to a British Christmas wherever it may be held.

" For five hours the company has been sitting round the table singing lustily; we haven't much talent, but everyone has contributed more or less, and the choruses are deafening. It is rather a surprising circumstance that such an unmusical party should be so keen on singing. On Christmas night it was kept up until 1 a.m."

Something of that sort is about to happen as I write this: behind the trenches in France or Mesopotamia, in camp at Salonika, in Egypt or Persia, on the North Sea, and on the Mediterranean, on troopships and in hospitals, Christmas will be celebrated with feasting and song. For there is nothing that links distant places and distant ages like Christmas music, and British manhood, never so scattered as now since Britain began, will, for a few hours, sing itself everywhere into touch again with the friends that are far and the days that are gone.

G

XVI

THE MECHANIC IN MUSIC

NOT the academic composer who laboriously lays out festival symphonies by the aid of a footrule and a book on orchestration, nor yet he who possesses a sort of mental mill for the production of drawing-room songs or anthems on the latest popular pattern—not these are in my mind at the moment. I mean the real mechanic, the man who thinks in terms of wood and metal, who is wise in pneumatics and on easy terms with electrics, who cons white drawings on blue paper and wipes his hands on a piece of cotton waste. For this individual has lately become a " force " in the musical world. Time was, I suppose, when music and mechanics had no dealings one with another, for time was, presumably, when no instrument existed but that which nature had given—the human voice. But the first of our rude ancestors who made a pipe and blew it, or stretched a string and twanged it, infringed the virgin virtue of the art. To put it bluntly, he introduced machinery.

From that day to this his descendants have carried on the work; from that day to this his pipe and string have been in course of evolution. Our flutes, our oboes, our clarinets and bassoons are

but the pastoral pipe brought into mechanical subjection. Our organ is but a combination of them
all, with a wonderful mechanical method of control. Our violins and violoncellos and our pianos
are merely the simple string multiplied in number,
reinforced in tone, and operated by means mechanical in a greater or less degree, according to the
nature of the effect desired.

Is music now passing too fully into the hands of
the mechanic? That is an often-mooted question
in this twentieth century. The violin, the oboe,
even the horn, which long rejoiced in what was
styled a "natural" condition, but now submits to
the government of a fearful and wonderful series
of valves and pistons—these, all, we accept as
legitimated by long use and old custom. Of the
piano, with its marvellously increased delicacy and
power of tone-variation, none complain. Even the
modern organ, with its four or five manuals, its
fifty or one hundred stops, its varying "wind
pressures," and its pistons, is an accredited member of the musical republic. But what of the
"piano-player," which puts within the plain man's
modest capacity the performance of a Liszt Rhap-
sody; the gramophone, which allows the arm-chair
critic to pronounce on the merits of Caruso or
Harry Lauder; the electrophone, which brings a
concert at the Queen's Hall, a musical comedy at
the Gaiety, or the Bach music at St. Anne's, Soho,
to the very fireside of the slacker or the bed of
the invalid? Is there in the realm of art such a
fiat as "Thus far shalt thou go and no further,"

and has science already overstepped its boundary line ?

Now, this is precisely the sort of question that is easy to ask but less so to answer. A whole class of artistic souls would reply in the affirmative; a great group of mechanics, manufacturers or merchants, in the negative. In both cases there is more than a mere ethical consideration involved; actual bread and butter is at stake, and some hold the view that Society's provision of this commodity is none too ample—that the success of the maker of piano-players means the starvation of the performer and the piano teacher.

XVII

A DEFENCE OF THE PIANO-PLAYER

IT is much easier to ask questions than to answer them. In the previous essay entitled "The Mechanic in Music," I essayed the easier task; now remains to me the harder. But to the large question, "Is music to-day passing too fully into the hands of the mechanic?" I cannot in brief space give a full reply. Instead I purpose to select one of the most striking manifestations of the mechanical spirit in the musical world, and say a word or two in its defence.

The last few years have seen a most remarkable development in the musical world. Within them have come to fruition the hopes and attempts of the inventors of a century past. At last there has been put upon the market a machine which will reproduce the works of composers, great and small, without demanding, on the part of its users, years of drudgery. This machine, to be quite frank, still has its enemies. Also it has many and warm friends. The difference of point of view which separates them is admirably set out in two letters which appeared in a well-known literary journal some time ago.

There one writer, in a broad and general way,

decried mechanical performance on the ground that it does not permit of that " emotional and artistic ' communion ' between the artist and the audience " which he feels to be essential, and which we all admit to be desirable. Music with him, that is to say, is not a mere matter of the production of so many tones in consecution and combination; it is a sort of conversation (not altogether one-sided either, by the way) between two people or bodies of people.

On the other hand, another writer maintained that we should " welcome all means whereby music —one of the best and most cosmopolitan influences in the world—may become free as air," and per-tinently added, " Why should the masterpieces of music be less available than those of literature ? "

The plain fact is, both of these gentlemen are right ! All art is of the nature of communication between the artist and the public, I suppose. And art certainly should be the possession, not of a cultured few, but of the great masses. If, then, we can find an instrument (a " machine," if you like) which, at one and the same time, permits the personal appeal of the artist and puts music within the reach of the many, both these writers mentioned above (and the large classes of the musical public of which they are very representa-tive) will presumably be satisfied.

Now I am admittedly selecting one feature of a big subject, and let it be clear that I am leaving on one side all *purely* mechanical means of tone production (if indeed there be such). The fact is that all makers of piano-players employ a useful individual called an advertising manager. And this gentleman is sometimes a little free in his statements. The piano-player that " a child can play in a quarter of an hour " I have personally never met with. My own instrument took a good deal of learning. It was at least a fortnight before I could accurately " hit " a note, and so take into my own control the amount of force with which the key was depressed. Once having gained that power, I found that I possessed almost (I do not say " quite ") as much ability to vary the degree of force and the degree of speed as the ordinary pianist could possibly have. And, after all, there is not much else in " expression " in performance than variation in these two particulars. That being so, I really do not see that the " communion " the first of our writers longs for is out of the question. It is true that sometimes I come across a bad " roll " (in my view the instruments are much better than the rolls, and great improvements must some day be made in the latter). Generally speaking, however, after a trial or two I can get the effect I want. Now what has been possible to me is, I suppose, possible to most. " The masterpieces of music," as our second correspondent puts it, are to me as much " available as those of literature." I can take a roll from my cabinet as I can take a book from my shelves. The latest rolls can be obtained, like the latest books, from a circulating library. Pieces that would otherwise have taken hours of practice before I could become really familiar with them (even were I a fine executant) I can now scrape acquaintance with in a quarter of an hour, and make into friends for life by repeated performances day after day for a week.

The piano-player has its drawbacks, of course, **and** these are *not* fully set out in the advertisements. But on the whole I agree with a lady reader (quite unknown to me) who, as I am told, went into a leading piano shop in London three days after an article of mine on piano-players had appeared in a certain weekly paper. She had been, she said, opposed to anything of a mechanical nature in musical performance, but was stimulated by the article to try to find out what sort of a performance could really be obtained by an up-to-date piano-player. Quite by chance I was in the same shop the next day and was told of her visit. It appears she heard an instrument well played by a member of the firm, and bought it on the spot. Like her, I am (on the whole) a convert to faith in the value of this particular manifestation of the activity of " The Mechanic in Music." Yet once I was an unbeliever.

XVIII

To-DAY the orchestra is being democratised. Haydn wrote symphonies for the court of a Prince, and Mozart for that of an Archbishop; now Strauss and Elgar write them for the "shilling public," and the Queen's Hall in autumn is thronged with middle-class music-lovers. Wise municipalities are beginning to promote orchestras, and the plain man knows his Beethoven and Wagner. This is a very plain chapter for that same plain man.

Now, roughly speaking, there are four ways of making musical sounds—by scraping, by blowing, by banging, and by plucking. Accepting this mode of classification, the instruments of the orchestra fall into four groups. A certain measure of the analytical faculty is necessary to the real enjoyment of art, and a recognition of the simple fact mentioned is the first step to the appreciation of orchestral music; but the recognition must not be merely the intellectual one of a fact, nor yet the visual one of the appearance of the instruments—it must also be aural. And in this last matter my chapter càn offer little help; I will only give one hint here—watch and listen during the "tuning-up."

(1). *The Strings.* The "bread and butter" of

the orchestra is the string group (the other groups are different kinds of cake). Here we have four different instruments—a family as it were, with the great double-bass for the gruff father, the graceful violoncello for the mother, and the viola and violin for boy and girl respectively. By another analogy they may be likened to a choir, the violins (first and second) corresponding with the sopranos and contraltos, the violas with the tenors, the violoncellos with the first basses, and the double-basses with the second basses. A word of explanation is necessary on this last point. In the older orchestral music (and that is what I have in mind in writing this very simple article) the violoncellos and double-basses play the same music, but the bigger bulk and longer strings of the latter result in their notes being an octave lower than those of the former.

The strings, of course, constitute the class which I have called the " scraping " instruments. On special occasions, however, the bow is laid aside and for the moment they become " plucking " instruments. Sometimes a small clamp, called a " mute," is applied to the bridge with the object of producing a particular ethereal effect.

(2). The *Wind Instruments* are divided into two sub-classes, according to their material—the wood and the brass. Of the wood-wind, the flute and its diminutive, the piccolo, are plain tubes, the clarinet has a mouthpiece with a single vibrating " reed " as the sound-producer (compare a toy trumpet with its single tongue of metal), and the oboe, the misnamed cor anglais and the bassoon constitute a little family in themselves, each having a double-reed mouthpiece (the equivalent of the *two* pieces of tin fastened together, with which boys imitate the Punch and Judy man). The brass instruments are simply tubes of varying shapes and sizes, with special mouthpieces for the production of sound. Inasmuch as a short tube produces a high sound, and a long one a low sound, some method has to be found of shortening and lengthening the tube so that all the notes of the scale may be available. In the case of horn and trumpet this is managed by the use of valves, which bring into use additional lengths of tube; in that of the trombone a pulling-out and pushing-in process takes place, with the same object.

(3). The chief *Percussion Instruments* (or bangers, as I have called them) are the big drum, with its indeterminate low note, the kettledrums, or timpani (really *musical* instruments these, capable of being exactly tuned to whatever notes the composer wishes for the moment), the clashing cymbals, which put the touch of red into the topmost chord of the climax, and the tinkling triangle. We will leave the tambourine out of account for the moment; it, nevertheless, sometimes has its artistic uses in the concert-hall, especially when the composer wishes to transport us to the Orient.

(4). The musical ministrations of David to Saul are to-day usually represented by the efforts of a lady performer, and she is the sole user of a "plucking" instrument, properly so to be called.

In listening to an orchestra it is convenient, as I have hinted, to regard the string family as supplying the staple of the tone. This family may be heard separately, or may have added to it one or more members of the wood-wind group. To these may be further added the brass (softly for romantic or solemn effects, loudly for bold and blatant ones). Or the wood-wind family or the brass may be heard alone, or one or more members of one family may be combined with one or more of another. A convenient figure of speech is that which describes the varying tones of the instruments in terms of colour, and the composer as holding a kaleidoscope which he may turn round and round, producing endless complexities of effect.

So ends this childishly simple description of a great engine of human emotion.

XIX

THE SYMPHONY

THEY call Haydn " Father of the Symphony," and the paternity cannot be denied. But behind the eighteenth-century Haydn there is a long line of ancestry that goes back right along the whole stream of existence of the human race—and perhaps further.

The summer of 1912, on one of the few fine days, I lay in a little wood on a Yorkshire moor and listened to the song of a bird. What its genus and species I do not know, but somewhere I have in musical notation a record of its performance. For this bird, having possibly a slightly more developed brain than some of its fellows, had discovered the principles upon which we humans construct all our music; in its song was to be found the essential basis of the music of Beethoven, Strauss, and Elgar.

To begin with, the bird was expressing its joy of life and its love of its mate, or some other of the feelings that in early summer animate the bird breast. And that is where Beethoven, Strauss, and Elgar begin—in personal expression. Music is the outcome of the need for sympathy; a bird

or a man feels so happy, or so sad, or so full of
some emotion, whatever it may be, that he must
tell the other members of his race. Primarily
music is personal expression, and this is the first
principle. Second, the joy or sorrow, or whatever
emotion may be felt, must be expressed in some
intelligible way : the material which springs to the
mind must be given out in some *order*.   In this
music does not differ from the other arts; in fact,
it has distinct resemblances to the most formal art
of all—that of architecture ("frozen music," some-
one has called this). It is useless for Tolstoi, in
his most inspiring "What is Art?" to speak as
though music were *merely* a matter of expression,
and as though the presence of formal beauty were
a negligible accident; expression and formal beauty
are twin sisters in the soul; one might almost say
that so far as art is concerned they are inseparable
Siamese twins.

Now the particular scheme of formal arrangement adopted by my feathered friend was this—
he sang one little phrase of three notes several
times, and then, before he or his auditors had time
to tire of it, took up another similar little phrase.
Presumably he had not the brain to be conscious
of what he was doing or why he was doing it;
but he had lighted upon the very principle that
lies at the foundation of all human music, and that
sharply distinguishes it, as a rule, from the music
of nature. For *nature music* (thunderings and
ripplings, the chirping of crickets and the song of
birds) and *art music* (songs and symphonies and

tone poems and fugues) differ chiefly in this, that in the latter case there is present the element of form and in the former case there is not.

There is a good and simple psychological explanation for this element of form in music. I can explain it best by two brief and well-known incidents. The first is that of the Scotsman who at a fair bought a dictionary (a dictionary is usually a rather big book for its price, and that may suggest his motive). Asked later by a friend how he was getting on with it, he replied that he had now read about half of it and only found one fault —it "changed the subject rather often." This constant change of subject was a mental tax, even to a member of an intellectual race. So in music a constant change of material would impose an excessive strain upon our listening powers. Phrase A, followed by phrase B, followed by phrase C, and so on through the alphabet, would tire us, however beautiful and expressive each of those phrases might be in itself. Constant variety may be enormously fatiguing, as anyone can witness who has attempted to follow a sermon which consisted merely of a string of irrelevant and unrelated pietudes.

The second illustration I draw from Besant and Rice's "The Golden Butterfly." The heroine of that novel, as may be remembered, had never entered a church until she was just leaving her teens. The lady who took her for the first time records: "I could have wished that her intensity of attitude had not betrayed a perfect absence of familiarity with church customs. During the psalms she began by listening with a little pleasure in her face. Then she looked a little bored; and presently she whispered to me, ' Dear Agatha, *I really must go out if the tune is not changed.*' " We who have been brought up from youth to occupy ourselves with rapt devotion during the singing of the Psalms of David can perhaps hardly realise the maddening effect of the reiteration of the ten-note melody of an Anglican chant upon a mind that still retained its power of criticism. Mere repetition is, then, quite insupportable in a musical composition considered as such, and returning to the sermon analogy once more, we may recall some sermon which persistently enforced some one point (possibly a good one), with never a digression from it, however momentary.

The main formal principle of the art of music is this—let there be variety, and let there be repetition. The theme may (indeed, *must*) be changed from time to time, but the thread of unity must run through the composition. It must be held together by the reappearance of former themes, whether in their old shape or some new one. This simple principle may be applied in an almost infinite number of ways.

I must now show its actual application in the detailed arrangement of the special type of composition mentioned in the title of this article.

There are in this world beautiful faces that tell of nothing behind them. And there are expressive faces that have little beauty. But the most attractive face of all is the one which is both expressive and beautiful.

In music it is easier to be beautiful than expressive. Hundreds of symphonies perfect in their formal arrangement have been composed; they pleased for the moment and were quickly forgotten. (The girl with a face, but no heart, may make a stir at twenty, but at forty she may be on the dusty shelf, nevermore to be taken down). A few symphonies have been composed that were stronger on the expressive side than on the formal. These stand a rather better chance of life, but their appeal can never be a wide one. It is the *combination* of expression and formal beauty that makes a work of art immortal. The artist must (first) have something to say, and (second) know how to say it.

People have now been composing symphonies for rather over a century and a half. That is not a large section of the world's existence, but already a great development has taken place. Roughly put, the direction of that development is from simplicity towards complexity. Haydn and Mozart, in the eighteenth century, expressed simple thoughts in a simple way. Beethoven, at the beginning of the nineteenth, expressed deeper thoughts in a more subtle way. Brahms, in the latter part of the nineteenth century carried this process yet farther, and Elgar, to-day, as I personally think, has carried it farther still. Thus symphonies are becoming harder to write and harder to hear. Haydn wrote one hundred and twenty, Beethoven nine, Brahms four; Elgar, so far, has only written two, and the man in the street often finds those beyond his comprehension for the moment.

A grasp of the formal principle is a great help to the understanding of a work of art.   Some happy folk have this grasp intuitively; others only possess it as the result of a struggle.   The reason a masterpiece makes its full appeal after several hearings is that then there has come about a sub-conscious conception of its parts and their relation to one another.   By previous study of the master-piece one might have given oneself the third-time appreciation at the first time of hearing.   This is the justification of the study of the formal side of music on the part of the concert-goer.

I have given the two principles of form as (a) unity and (b) variety.   The former is obtained by the repetition of themes, and the latter by their alternation.   Let us see how these principles apply in the first " movement " of a Haydn symphony. (A symphony is a big piece made by putting to-gether four smaller ones; these latter are called " movements.").

A very little examination will show us that the whole movement is made out of two chief themes. Further inspection will show us that these two themes are contrasted in character; probably the first is bold and masculine, and the second grace-ful and feminine (here the symphony and the novel own the same principle—one apparently essential in human life). At the outset the themes are simply "given out," separated by a passage which serves to connect them—to lead from one to the other. (This "giving out" constitutes the first section of the movement, perhaps, roughly, a third of it in length). Next, we find the themes are "developed," *i.e.*, they undergo all manner of changes, brief passages being taken from one or the other and treated in a variety of ways and in a number of keys. (This "development" constitutes the second section of the movement, and occupies, probably, roughly, another third of the time of performance). By-and-by we come to the final section, the "recapitulation," or repetition of the themes. This is merely a repetition of the first section, with some possible trifling alterations and an important one. This latter is a change of key. In the first section it will be found that the two subjects are in different keys from one another, yet keys that the ear feels to be nearly related. In the second section the fragmentary treatment of the subjects (or "development") takes us through many changes of key, some of them, possibly, remote; in the last section the two subjects are in the same key as one another—the principal key of the piece, the one with which it opened. Again there is close analogy with the novel. Think of the first (generally bold and masculine) subject as the hero, and the second (generally graceful and feminine) subject as the heroine. At the opening we make their acquaintance in opposing moods; in the middle we find them passing through all manner of vicissitudes; in the last they have come to the same way of thinking—significantly, that of the hero. (Perhaps Dr. Ethel Smyth, Suffragette and eminent composer, will one day show us how a symphony may be written in which the key of the second subject may triumph).

The principles of unity and variety are evident in the above treatment. The second, third, and fourth " movements " of the symphony show us the same principles, possibly applied in some different way. Probably the second movement is a slow one, very likely either on the above plan or some modification of it, or simply an air with a series of variations (unity and variety again). The third is likely to be a minuet and trio (*i.e.*, simply two minuets arranged first minuet, second minuet, first minuet—unity and variety once more, this time on the sandwich plan). The last may be a rondo, *i.e.*, a principal theme returning over and over again, its repetitions separated one from another by other matter (unity and variety in another obvious form). The whole symphony may be preceded by a brief slow introduction, intended to prepare the mind, to tune up the audience, as it were.

So much for the simple Haydn symphony. Readers who are pianists should get a cheap volume of Haydn's or Mozart's symphonies (solo or duet arrangement), and play it through. Haydn's *Paukenwirbel* (drum-roll) symphony is a good and attractive example. It may be known by the roll on a low note which commences it, and gives it its nickname.

XX

THE FUGUE AND THE PLAIN MAN

" A FUGUE," says some American humorist, " is a piece in which the voices come in one by one—and the people go out one by one." The first statement of this definition is undeniable, and the latter embodies more than a morsel of truth, for, as many an organist can tell you, the after-service fugue quickly empties the church. The fugue makes a good " playing-out " piece.

The musician revels in fugues; following Schumann's advice, he makes Bach his Bible. The plain man tells us that nothing bores him so quickly; for him no music that exists savours so much of the " classical " (hated word!).——Why this sharp divergence of taste?

The fact is that the musician is in possession of two or three simple little facts that are unsuspected by the plain man; with these to guide him, he knows *how to listen*. Here are these facts : let the plain man grasp them and listen accordingly, and, with a little perseverance in applying them, he too will gain pleasure from the fugue.

(1) To begin with, the fugue is essentially choral in style : often it is actually written for voices (*e.g.*, some of Handel's choruses); but even when written

for instrumental performance it keeps strictly to a certain number of " parts," and the analogy actually leads to these being styled " voices." So, whether the fugue be vocal or instrumental, we speak of it as being " in three voices," or " in four voices," and so forth. This choral character is the first great fact to be grasped: to some extent, at any rate, we must hear these separate " parts " or " voices," and be able to distinguish one from another, just as in a chorus we might give our attention now to the tenor, now to the soprano, etc., as one voice or the other became, for the moment, the most important of the four engaged.

(2) The next great characteristic is this—the fugue is founded upon a " subject," just as a sermon is founded on a text. The fugue begins with this " subject," and often ends with it; and right through the piece this simple little melodic phrase is to be heard, tossed about from one " voice " to another. If the listener knows no more than these two basic little facts he is better equipped than ninety-nine out of a hundred of his fellow-listeners, and will gain an enormous advantage over them in the pleasure he will experience as the fugue is performed.

(3) The opening of a fugue is decidedly peculiar, and oftentimes, in itself, might appear singularly ineffective. For *one voice alone* gives out the subject—a simple little line of single notes such as a child might play with one finger. But this plain little phrase is soon taken up by another voice (the

first voice meanwhile supplying a sort of em-
broidery to it). Then a third voice takes it up
(whilst the other two " embroider "); then a fourth
(whilst the three " embroider "). If the fugue be
a five-part of six-part fugue, this process is carried
further. Alternately these entries of the subject
are in the chief key of the piece, and in a contrasting key, so that we get a sort of see-saw from
key C (it may be) to key G, and back to key C
again. The technical term for an entry in the
contrasting key is " Answer "—we say the subject is in C, the answer in G, and so on. Here
is Robert Browning's description of the fugue up
to this point :—

> " First you deliver your phrase—
>   Nothing propound, that I see,
> Fit in itself for much blame or much praise—
>   Answered no less, where no answer need be ;
> Off start the two on their ways.

> " Straight must a Third interpose,
>   Volunteer needlessly help—
> In strikes a Fourth, a Fifth thrusts in his nose,
>   So the cry's open, the kennel's a-yelp,
> Argument's hot to the close ! "

(4) This stage concluded, the human craving for
variety demands satisfaction, and an " Episode "
occurs. This is nothing but a brief passage of
the nature of relief from the repeated statement
and counter-statement of subject and answer. Probably, however, it is made out of fragments of the
previous matter, and in this respect it bears a re-

semblance to the " development " portion of the Symphony (see page 99).

(5) Then come further entries of the subject, this time in some other key, into which the Episode has cleverly led us. After this a further Episode, and further entries—and so on, until we draw to the close of the piece, which brings us home again to the key from which we set out, the chief key of the piece.

Other mysteries there are to unfold, of course, but the above simple statement is all the plain man requires at the outset. And this is avowedly a plain man's chapter.

It will be seen that the dual principle of construction alluded to in my treatment of the Symphony as underlying all musical composition is to be found here—unity *plus* variety. The application of this principle is, however, quite different. A little confusion may perhaps be avoided if it be pointed out that the term " subject " carries in the symphony the significance of a more or less extended passage (it may be even a page or more in length), whereas in the fugue it means simply a brief phrase, in one voice or part at a time, *i.e.*, purely melodic in character. This is, perhaps, one of the many absurdities of technical musical nomenclature.

Finally, a word of advice may be given—concentrate for a time upon the purely intellectual and formal aspect of listening, as outlined above. Then, as, with practice, this becomes sub-conscious, you will discover that the fugue has also its emotional side. All that I have done is to describe the body. The soul defies description, but will reveal itself.

XXI

THE VIRTUE OF BREVITY

AN APPEAL TO THE COMPOSER

THE other day, in a certain daily paper, I was rude to one of our most eminent critics, Mr. Ernest Newman. He had been writing very hopelessly about the prospects of British music, and I called him " a musical Pro-German." I fear the words rankled, for I see that he has since used a page and a quarter to show that he is no Pro-German but that I am a guttersnipe. Thus does rudeness breed rudeness, but there is this consolation, that our terms of opprobrium may now be considered to have " cancelled out." When we next take up the matter we shall be able to do so with a clean slate.

It was really the more important to shun personalities because the subject matter of our discussion was of importance. Is British music to gain a firmer footing as a by-result of the present war?

That our British composers have been doing increasingly good work during the last three decades or so, no one can deny, but shall we be able to shake out of the mind of the big public the last lingering remains of the idea that the best music necessarily comes from Germany? Obviously that depends largely on the British composer, and with all the impertinence he is accustomed to expect from a music critic, I want to offer him a little advice. It is not exactly new, but its frequent repetition seems called for. Its tenor is " be brief ! "

Mozart and Schumann have already expounded this principle in writing of music, Edgar Allan Poe, in his essay, " On the Principles of Composition," has shown its application in poetry, and thousands have felt its force as regards sermons.

" Our taste in Germany," said Mozart, " is for long things, but short and good is better." Those composers came in for Schumann's heavy condemnation " who squeeze the last drop out of their themes and spoil their good ideas by tiresome thematic treatment." (Schumann, by the way, did not always practise what he preached; in effect, he strengthened his case by a few practical examples of the evil he denounced).

Now, whatever good things I may have previously said about modern British music, it must be admitted that with that numerous personage, " the man in the street," it is still on its trial. I do not believe that man is conscious of any real feeling against it, but a positive affection has still to be won. We should all like him to recognise that British self-expression requires British music; we should like him to cultivate a spirit of national pride, and when he sees a concert bill to say,

" Hello, a new British symphony. *I must hear that!* " The trouble is that in matters of art few people do a thing because they ought, and many because they like. The man in the street must then be taught to like British music.

Not one person in ten really "likes" a new symphony or tone-poem the first time he hears it. The expenditure of brain power in taking in a new work on symphonic scale is too great. A weariness creeps over one, and the piece which began so brightly begins to bore. This was a frequent experience at the British Music Festival a short time ago. Again and again did one feel that a good thing had been spoiled by the generosity of its composer.

Then (and this must be mentioned with delicacy) it is so much easier to write effectively in the short forms than in the long ones. Composition, like any other art, calls for experience, and opportunities of hearing their works are so rare still for our younger men that by the time they are fifty they will have gained less knowledge of how their music sounds than Haydn or Mozart had at twenty-five. Let them, then, choose the easier part, and not be ashamed of it; they will climb the higher.

Further, a short piece needs less rehearsal, and if the young man wants conductors to give his works a chance that is a great consideration. Then the concert giver is asked to speculate far less heavily when he has a short piece put before him. If a piece has taken forty-five or fifty minutes, and proved a failure, the audience is resentful; whereas, if it has taken only ten minutes nobody thinks any more about it. (Incidentally this is a gain to the unfortunate composer. He is not for ever damned; people have not scored up his failure against him).

Lastly, there is a far greater chance of getting a short work published than a long one, and everyone admits that one of the greatest disadvantages under which our young British school labours is that its works have not yet, in any quantity, passed under the printing-press, and cannot therefore become widely dispersed.

Really, as I have written this I have become so warmed to my subject that I find myself wishing that the Chancellor of the Exchequer, in his last Budget, had put a heavy tax on new pieces of orchestral music of over seven and a half minutes in length, with a crushing super-tax on those over fifteen. In ten years' time the tax would have been withdrawn, and the symphonies and hour-long tone-poems might have been again begun. Hundreds of present-day concert-goers would have rejoiced at the Chancellor's action, and future generations would have arisen and called him blessed.

XXII

MUSIC FROM THE HEBRIDES

In the Isles there still live—fairies! Perhaps that is one reason why some of the most lovely tunes in the world come from there. "The fairy folk," says Kenneth Macleod, "are so good at the music that if thou wert to enter the 'bruth' to-day, the sapling might become the tallest tree in the forest ere thou wouldst get tired of listening. Hast heard of Cnoc-na-piobaireachd, the knoll-of-piping, in Eigg? In my young days, and in the young days of the ones before me, all the lads of the island used to go there on the beautiful moonlight nights, and, bending down an ear to the knoll, it was tunes they would get, and tunes indeed: reels that would make the Merry-dancers themselves go faster, and laments that would draw tears from the eyes of a corpse: sure, in one night, a lad o'music might get as many reels and laments as would marry and bury all the people in Eigg—ay, and in the whole Clanranald country forbye!"

It is not a "lad o'music," but a Celtic woman musician, Mrs. Kennedy-Fraser, who has taken up the task of gathering the music. And not only marrying and burying music, "reels and laments," has she brought us, but spinning songs, milking songs and churning songs, maiden songs and mother songs, rowing songs and reiving songs, love songs and songs of death. Some, it may be, come from the " wee folk " of " the knoll-of-piping." Others are memories of the old pagan priests. Still others tell of the dawn of Christianity in the Isles, for perhaps we have a link with the old Celtic Church, with Iona and St. Columba, in such a song as the traditional " Dawn Prayer " of the Clanranalds.

For the last forty years enthusiasts have been working for the salvation of our fast-decaying national folk-song, and the last ten years or so have seen its recognition by publishers and public, educationalists and composers. The folk-song and folk-dance movements have happily coincided with a growth of national feeling in music.

It is foolish, even in wartime, to cast stones at the Germans' music simply because during two centuries it has been better than ours. For two centuries before that ours was better than theirs; indeed, as a matter of plain historical fact, theirs is based largely on ours. The genius of music flits from country to country, and from race to race. Our turn has been, and perhaps it is to come again.

One thing is certain, however, whilst the nations, one after another, seize the torch, and in due season pass it on, it can only burn brightly in the hands of those who can feed its flame with the oxygen of strong national feeling. The Russians have felt this so strongly that in their efforts

to develop a real Russian School, they have deliberately cast on one side a great deal of the work
of the Germans, from Bach to Beethoven. Stravinsky, for instance, almost appears to derive from
no one and to come from nowhere. He has taken
something like a fresh start, and so far has he
gone that I remember that he once actually told
me (this is to report blasphemy, but I do so in
a confidential whisper!) that nothing of Bach ap-
pealed to him and hardly anything of Beethoven.
Perhaps we may see later that he has owed more
than he thought to Bach and to Beethoven, but
there it is—an attempt to be his own individual
and national living Russian self; a fear of becoming a pale bloodless Beethoven.

We, on our part, long for a true British school
of music. How are we to get it? By soaking
our composers in folk-song, say some. The Russians, whose music is more and more proving its
independent quality and serious value, did that.
At first the Russian composers wove their compositions (operatic and symphonic) out of their
national song: then, later, having by this means
cleansed their creative minds of German and Aus-
trian idiom, they ceased to use folk-material, no
longer needing it.

It is Mr. Edwin Evans' view, as expressed lately
in several articles, that this plan should be ours
too, and to some extent our composers have already
adopted it. Stanford and Mackenzie, for instance,
have used Irish and Scottish themes respectively.
Vaughan Williams has written Norfolk Rhap-

sodies; W. G. Whittaker has made wonderful choral arrangements of Northumbrian tunes. Rutland Boughton, I believe, was the inventor of this form of composition. Percy Grainger has used some actual folk-themes, and other themes in British folk-tune idiom, in piano and orchestral works. These are but random examples from a large number of cases.

Now Granville Bantock is at work on the Hebridean tunes. His beautiful choral treatment of the " Mermaid's croon " has just come to hand; he has lately produced a large orchestral work upon themes from Mrs. Kennedy-Fraser's collection. This is surely as it should be. British themes for British composers! We have realised, to our surprise, that our islands possess a folk-tune treasury comparable with any in the world, and the purest gold amongst it, as I think, is that which comes from the Isles.

XXIII

DICKENS AND MUSIC

In these hero-worshipping days the slightest par-
ticle of personal and intimate information concerning the great ones of the earth is a welcome possession. Let us, then, be thankful that the precise
character of Landor's snore has been put on record
for us (and for generations yet unborn) by the
very descriptive pen of his friend Charles Dickens.
Here it is: "That steady snore of yours, which I
once heard piercing the door of your bedroom
. . . . reverberating along the bell-wire in the hall,
so getting outside into the street, playing Æolian
harps among the area railings, and going down
the New Road like the blast of a trumpet."

Now to whom but a musician would such a series
of metaphors and similes have occurred?   Of
course, in our younger days, we are all musicians,
whether we wish it or not, and Dickens was no
exception; at the Wellington House Academy, in
the Hampstead Road, he learnt his five-finger
exercises on the piano and received some teaching
on the violin. Unlike some of us, however, he
did not let these early trials embitter him, and
years after, on the occasion of his first voyage to
America, we find him still a performer—on the

accordion! It seems that on this last-named instrument he played *Home, Sweet Home* every
night for the benefit of the ladies' cabin, "and
pleasantly sad it makes us." Something of the
effect of these performances may, of course, have
been due to the appropriate choice of the music,
and the same may be said of those of a later
voyage, when, with the captain, "a Chicago lady,
and a strong-minded woman from I don't know
where," he made up a vocal quartet. "We sang,"
he says, "*Auld Lang Syne,* with a tender melancholy expressive of having all four been united
from our cradles. The more dismal we were, the
more delighted the company were. Once (when
we paddled i' the burn) the captain took a little
cruise round the compass on his own account,
touching at the *Canadian Boat Song,* and taking
in supplies at *Jubilate."* So Dickens was more
than a mere listener; obeying the apostolic injunc-
tion (which may surely have its application in the
musical world), he became not a mere hearer,
"but a doer also."

Shakespeare's many references to music have
prompted several books; those of Dickens have
brought forth one. I commend it to lovers of
music who are also lovers of Dickens. It is called
Charles Dickens and Music, and its author, Mr.
J. T. Lightwood, has made in it a notable collection of references to music in the novels and other
writings. There is, for instance, the theatre orchestra in *Nicholas Nickleby,* which consisted
of three fiddles, and played "a variety of popular

airs, with involuntary variations," and that other one at Mrs. Gattleton's private theatricals (*Sketches by Boz*). Of a performance of this latter it is said: " The overture, in fact, was not unlike a race between the different instruments; the piano came in first by several bars, and the violoncello next, quite distancing the poor flute; for the deaf gentleman *too-too'd* away, quite unconscious that he was at all wrong, until apprised, by the applause of the audience, that the overture was concluded." Then (in *Dombey and Son*) we find Mr. Morfin, who was not only a 'cellist, meeting certain friends weekly for the performance of " quartets of the most tormenting and excruciating nature," but also an expert whistler, who on one occasion went " accurately through the whole of Beethoven's 'Sonata in B '" (a sonata, by the way, which is not to be found in any of the professedly complete editions of the composer's works!) Fortunately, Mr. Morfin's landlady was deaf, and his violoncello performances only produced in her " a sensation of something rumbling in her bones," which was a merciful dispensation of nature.

Reliable statisticians tell us that nearly forty instruments are mentioned by Dickens and well over a hundred different songs. These figures are respectable, of course, and with them, to his credit, Dickens probably outdistances most other English novelists, so far as musical allusions are concerned. The real point lies, however, in the apt use he has made of such musical knowledge as he possessed.

Sometimes, it is true, he gets astray, as when he unwittingly creates a phenomenon in the shape of a boy of fourteen with a tenor voice. Generally, however, he is correct, and it is not at all astonishing to find, from Mr. Francesco Berger's reminiscences, lately published, that in the specially constructed private theatre at the rear of the novelist's house in Tavistock Square, he was wont to employ " a small but efficient orchestra."

In closing a too short chapter on a large subject it is fitting that I should, at any rate, recall to my readers' memories that it was Mrs. Micawber's vocal interpretations that attracted her future husband's attention " to an extraordinary degree " (so that, in his own words, he " resolved to win that woman or perish in the attempt "), that Tom Pinch was an organist, that Mr. Dombey's second marriage was celebrated by the performances of a brass band and of the " marrow bones and cleavers," that Frederick Dorrit was a clarinettist, and that the elder Weller's plan for liberating from the Fleet the immortal Mr. Pickwick was to carry him out in a piano. " There ain't no vurks to it. It 'ull hold him easy, vith his hat and shoes on; and breathe through the legs, vich is holler."

XXIV

THE CARILLONS OF BELGIUM

THE bell is the only musical instrument that can be heard by a whole town at one time. Bell music is public as is no other music. It is community music.

How is it, then, that this country, with all its musical activities, has developed bell music to so small a degree, whilst Belgium and Holland have made it such a feature of the life of the people? Here, with us, bell music means, at the best, change-ringing—excellent muscular exercise for a little band of enthusiasts, but a very rudimentary form of art, partaking of the nature of mathematics as much as of music. In Belgium bell-ringing means the Carillon, with its mechanically played tunes, that tell the hours and their halves and quarters as they pass, and its skilled human playing, by means of keyboard and pedal board, at certain fixed times of the day or week. At the highest, our bell music is on the level of intelligent peasant performance. Theirs in Belgium calls for the exercise of actual conscious musicianship, often of a very high order.

We have in this country, it is true, a few carillons, only five in number, I believe—Aberdeen, Bournville, Cattistock (Dorset), Eaton Hall (Cheshire), and Loughborough. The largest (and possibly the best) of these is the last named, with its forty bells. In Belgium almost all towns of size have their carillons, and a large and efficient class of musicians exists whose skill is directed to their use.

A visit to a Belgian carillon chamber is an interesting experience. Well do I remember climbing painfully to the top of the famous belfry of Bruges. There sat the town carillonneur, with a double keyboard before him, not unlike that of a two-manual organ, and a pedal-board that increased the similarity. But the manner of performance was different enough, for each note called, not for the gentle pressure of the organ touch, but for a powerful blow with fist or foot, the former protected by a thick leather pad. It was tiring, thirsty work, only to be undertaken with the coat off and the sleeves rolled up.

The biggest, deepest bells are naturally those played by the feet, the manual keyboards being connected with the smallest ones. Music in three parts is very commonly played, and chords of four notes are by no means out of the question. As Mr. William Graham Rice points out, however, in his recent book (" Carillons of Belgium and Holland," John Lane), of which this chapter is in a sense a review, the greatest care is taken in the disposition of the notes of a chord. Overtones are a prominent feature of bell tone, as anyone who has listened to even the single bell of an

English village church must have noticed, and two low notes together from a carillon would be as unpleasant as two neighbouring low notes on the piano, struck with the damper pedal down. It may be of interest to say that when the carillon is played automatically, as at the hours and their quarters, the bells are struck on their outer surface by hammers actuated by a cylinder like that of a musical box. When, however, the carillonneur is present, and the playing is from the keyboard, the inside of each bell is struck by a clapper connected by simple mechanism with its proper key of the keyboard. If the Belgian carillonneurs are finer than those of Holland, it is largely because this connecting mechanism is more direct and better contrived. In Belgium, carillon making and carillon playing have reached their highest points.

Ask the man in the street the derivation of the word "belfry," and he will say at once it is from the word "bell." Strange as it may seem, this is not so. "Bergen" to protect and "Fridu," peace, security, are the roots of the word. And a belfry was a symbol of freedom. Here is an extract from Grant Allen's "The European Tour," emphasizing the point :—

"These Flemish belfries are in themselves very interesting relics, because they were the first symbols of corporate existence and municipal power which every town wished to erect in the Middle Ages. The use of the bell was to summon the citizens to arms in defence of their rights, or to counsel for their common liberties. Every burgher community desired to wring the right of erecting such a belfry from its feudal lord; and those of Bruges and Ghent are still majestic memorials of the freedom-loving wool-staplers of the thirteenth century. By the side of the belfry stood the Cloth Hall, representing the trade from which the city derived its wealth."

A Belgian belfry belongs to the municipality, and the bell master is a municipal officer. Even when hung in a church tower, it is the municipality that controls the carillon. The management of the bells is civic, and if the religious element enters, it does so in a subordinate fashion.

Here is an example for our own country when the happy times of peace arrive, and public money begins to flow once again into channels of public utility. There is as much justification, surely, for muncipal carillons as for parks, free libraries, or art galleries, and more than for free organ recitals. As regards the participants in the production of art, that sturdy British institution, the choral society, is the most democratic activity existing; as regards the size and constitution of the audience the Belgian carillon takes the palm.

It is worthy of remark, by the way, that the most popular piece of fine music our country has produced for many years is " Carillon," a *pièce d'occasion* that is, for once, a real work of genius. Under the whole fabric of this composition runs a " ground bass " (as the musician would call it), in this case a plain, simple half-scale of four descending notes, repeated in varying rhythm time after time. Thus Elgar, in his tribute to Belgium, has taken an English chime, rather than a Belgian carillon, as his " motif."   But the result is so magnificently, thrillingly effective, that who can cavil ?

NOTE.—It is interesting to observe that the earliest piece of English art-music on record (see the account of *Sumer is icumen in* on pages 9 and 10) and one of the latest, both use the device of the " ground-bass."   Intermediately Purcell employed it magnificently in many compositions.

XXV

How little do Englishmen know about their national music! How little do they realise the position their past entitles them to take up and the airs they are entitled to display in view of the great deeds of their musical ancestors! Sometimes it almost seems as though, like Uriah Heep, they rejoice in being " very 'umble."

"No original painting, no original music, were cradled in Tudor England." That is a sweeping statement, and it is made by one who writes with great authority upon the period in question. I read it a few months ago in a British Academy lecture on "Shakespeare and the Italian Renaissance," and have spent the time since in gathering courage to oppose its author. The statement is but one more example of our most unbecoming national humility in musical matters.

Its author is our great Shakespeare expert; the standard work on Shakespeare is his, and its recent new edition has placed him, if possible, still higher in the estimation of every student of English literature. The lightest word he may utter about Shakespeare or the England of Shakespeare's days is likely to reverberate for a long time in the pages of those lesser authors who make their books out of the writings of the greater ones. It becomes a duty, therefore, if one has evidence against any one of his statements to put it forth.

This is a time when we are all feeling so very patriotic that anything we may say in favour of our own country is probably subject to some discount. Already, in a previous chapter in this volume, I have briefly alluded to the doings of English composers during the Tudor period. This time I will leave my own views largely on one side and quote from a German writer, Professor Johannes Wolf, of Berlin. For the most part he refers to the very period mentioned :—

" We know the praise of Erasmus, who said that the English challenged the prerogative of being the most accomplished in music of any people. More than thirty years before Buus, Willaert, and Bendusi, who began the evolution of Italian clavier music at Venice, England had an excellent composer for the virginals in Hughe Ashton. Already, about 1510, his compositions show that element highly developed which demands our peculiar consideration in the English virginal music; the variation, especially of songs and dances. The researches of historians have established the great influence that this technique of the English virginalists produced on the art of the Continent, at first on the music of the Netherlands. Dr. John Bull and Peter Philips, two excellent masters, were those who interposed; Jan Pieter Sweelinck was their docile disciple, and his school was of the greatest importance for Northern Germany through his pupils Scheidt, Scheidemann, Praetorius, Schildt and Siefert.

"This English virginal music seems to be original; the works of Byrd, Bull, Orl. Gibbons, Morley, Farneby, and later of Purcell, are worthy of our greatest attention. In these small musical pictures we are surprised at the richness of fancy, the delicacy of the ornaments, the character of the melodic line, and often the audacity of the harmony. Just in harmonic relation, we cannot but admire the art of Dr. Bull, especially in his first hexachord fancy, which may be compared with Bach's grand art in the *Well-tempered Clavier.* In general, here we find the fundaments of clavier-technique."

Professor Wolf is quite right in his last statement, quoted above. It would be literally true to say that Bach, Mozart, Beethoven, and Chopin built upon an English foundation.

When he comes to the English choral music of the end of the Tudor period Professor Wolf is just as ungrudging, and, as a matter of fact, he has every musical historian of importance at his back in every assertion he makes.

"The great period of English instrumental practice was also the golden age of vocal music. Let us only touch the characteristic forms. It is true that the madrigal is not an original fruit of the tree of English art, and has not enjoyed a long life in the British Isles, and yet the specimens of Morley, Dowland, Weelkes, Benet, Gibbons belong to the best that has been ever created in this form, and are, after a life of three hundred years, as fresh as in their first days. There is, for instance, not any madrigal better known than the *Fire! Fire!* of Morley. A great part of these songs have become the property of the German choirs."

" The madrigal is not an original fruit of the tree of English art," says the professor. This is true enough, and the same words might be used of the sonnet. In each case England took a form of art from Italy, but quickly breathed into it the national spirit, and made it a means of English artistic expression.

I had meant to quote also from eminent Belgian and Danish writers, but there is no space, without lengthening this chapter unduly, to do more than give the German professor's forecast of our musical future.

"We hear in these days the musical emanations of many periods of English history, and we are ravished. A nation that is so rich in beautiful music, and has advanced the evolution of music in the way the English have done belongs to the elect. It is true that in the last two centuries other nations have had the leading position, but once, and perhaps soon, the call will sound again : ' English musicians to the front !'   We know the English love of music, we know their work in the past and in the present, and with full conviction and joy we join in the poet's words :—

Blessed England, full of melody."

So much for a German view of musical England.

XXVI

THE WORST TAUGHT SUBJECT

AN AUTUMN REFLECTION

THE middle of September has arrived, and at every London station fond mothers will soon be bidding good-bye to their boys and girls; then, for nearly three months, London middle and upper class homes will be empty of children from twelve to eighteen. Now, one question that is being asked in a good many homes, with all the pathos of which the youthful voice is capable, is this: " *Need* I take music this term ? " The moment, as it probably happens, is propitious for a favourable reply. Father is thinking of coming taxation, that is to rob him, he hears, of just a trifle more than the actual amount of his income, and he may overrule mother for once. Now it is a sad thing to say, but in a good many cases the only loser by father's compliance will be—the music teacher.

Of all the subjects in the school curriculum, music is probably still the worst taught. Things have been improving during the last twenty years (and still more during the last ten), but over the whole subject lies the fatal influence of a bygone tradition—that of the " accomplishment." Education has taken such a different trend during the last generation, that it may be doubted whether this tradition lingers anywhere else in the curriculum; but here it is still all-powerful. The old idea of training our daughters to shine in the drawing-room may have weakened, but the schoolmistress and the parent still look upon music lessons as a preparation for performance. Every one knows, of course, that not one-half of the children who learn the piano ever touch the instrument in after life. Their music teachers, most of all, realise that hours weekly are being wasted. We all know that music is one of life's graces, but it has occurred to few that there is any other way of conferring it upon a child than through the imperfect medium of its own stumbling fingers. Those fingers are better trained now than ever before, for the pedagogy of pianism has now been taken in hand, and teachers are expected to have definite ideas as to their aims and methods. Better music is in use, too. No longer does Dorothy come home at the term's end prepared to entertain her aunts with some cheaply strung together variations on *Home, Sweet Home.* The *Bird Waltz* has vanished, and *The Battle of Prague* can only be fought again by those who care to rummage amongst the bound volumes of music that remain as relics of grandmother's school-days. But Dorothy still " learns music," and learning music still means scales and arpeggios, sonatinas, a Chopin Waltz, one of the easier Beethoven sonatas, and—an examination certificate of " The

K

Associated Board (patron: His Majesty the King)."

Now these things are not to be too lightly regarded. Dorothy *may* be really musical, she *may* have fingers that are capable of learning to express her very soul in waves of sound. But if that be the case it is ten to one that her sisters are not so gifted. As for her brothers, I regret to say that the closely fitted school time-table, with its provision for each moment both of lesson-hours and of play-hours, allows far too little music-time for the ordinary human boy ever to progress much beyond the stage of execution requisite for a simple waltz on week-days and a hymn tune in two flats or three sharps on Sundays. If Dorothy and her younger sisters and brothers really have the native ability and the native perseverance, by all means let them learn. But is there no better way of tackling the subject with school-children in the mass?

Well, what is done in literature? Dorothy learns poetry, but there is no expectation of turning her into an elocutionist. She is introduced to Shakespeare, but there is no attempt to make her an actress. The aim of the teaching she gets is to bring her into touch with a great humanising influence in the Drama. She may, it is true, be asked to recite a poem, or to take part in a school play, but the ideal is that she should learn to appreciate literature. With this in view she has presented to her not second or third rate stories (much piano " teaching-music " is but third rate) but masterpieces. That teacher is thought the most successful whose pupils leave school with a real and abiding love of literature and a passable standard of taste.

Surely this is what we want in music, too. Shocking as it may seem, hundreds of children "learn music" for the length of their school life and never hear a masterpiece, and indeed, hear no music at all except such as their own untrained musical sense and half-trained fingers can compass.

But things are looking up. Already in a few schools the "appreciation lesson" has become a feature of the time-table. The big public schools have their organ recitals and their orchestras. Music lectures and concerts are common. A love of music is worth any amount of five-finger exercises, and the capacity to enjoy a symphony is beyond all examination certificates. But perhaps I have gone too far in condemning the child's personal practice. Scripture gives me just the expression I want and there can be no impropriety in applying it in such a worthy cause. As concerns piano-teaching on the one hand, and "appreciative" teaching on the other, it will be best to put it: "This should ye do, and not leave the other undone."

XXVII

THE AGINCOURT SONG

IT is five hundred years since, in the grey hour before dawn, the priests of Henry V said Mass in his camp; since, after his own long and fervid prayer, the King went forth to marshal his army; since the English arrows played such havoc in the ranks of the French horsemen, struggling to free themselves from the clinging autumn mud. Five hundred years since, casting aside their bows, our archers drew out their leaden mallets and crushed in the iron helmets of the foe; five hundred years since, in a wild confusion, the enemy fled and scattered; since the priests who had gathered in the dawn to sing Mass gathered again at the end of the day to sing " Non nobis " and " Te Deum."

A special interest clings about the tradition of the twenty-fifth of October, 1415, for the deeds of that day gave us one of our finest national songs. Perhaps, as Mr. Geoffrey Shaw was saying recently, the famous Agincourt song ought to be made the National Anthem of England. It has a quality that is truly English, a straightforwardness of style, a melodic curve of wide range (like so many of the finest old English songs), a rhythm that tells of vigour and self-reliance, of enterprise and strength. There is something about it that calls for men's voices, hundreds of them, and brazen tones from a large band. Were it not that it is so entirely English, that it has so little in its quality or its associations for Scotsmen or Irishmen, it would be the very thing for the celebration of victory in these, our own days—half a thousand years after its composition.

As for the words of the Agincourt Song, surely Bishop Percy is too modest, when, in his " Reliques," he gives them " merely as a curiosity." " Homely rhymes " he calls them, but they ring with rejoicing and martial ardour :—

> " Owre kynge went forth to Normandy,
> With grace and mygt of chivalry ;
> The God for hym wrougt marvelously,
> Wherefore Englonde may calle, and cry
> Deo gratias :
> Deo gratias Anglia redde pro victoria.

> " Now gracious God he save owre kynge,
> His peple, and all his wel wyllynge,
> Gef him gode lyfe, and gode endynge,
> That we with merth mowe savely synge
> Deo gratias :
> Deo gratias Anglia redde pro victoria."

Who wrote the Agincourt Song? Nobody knows for certain. Perhaps one of the fifteen minstrels who accompanied Henry V. to France, receiving as their guerdon twelve pence a day. The King, says Holinshed, would not suffer " ditties to be made and sung by minstrels of his glorious victory; for that he would whollie

have the praise and thankes altogether given to
God." But the Agincourt Song as it has come
down to us, is perhaps not a " ditty " within " the
meaning of the Act "; is it not rather a hymn ?

There are some who think that John of Dunstable wrote the song. This is likely enough.
The musical treatises of the day speak of this
composer not merely as a great English musician,
but as the greatest musician of any country at
that time. It seems certain that by his skill he
turned music into straighter channels, lifted
musical composition at last to the level of an art:

Surely such a man must have been in favour
with the music-loving king! Surely he was at-
tached to the newly-founded Chapel Royal! Surely they would call upon him, of all men, to arrange
music for London's welcome of the victor of Agincourt! Perhaps, as Mr. Henry Davey suggests,
he passed over again into Normandy · with the
king, sang at the head of the processions before
him in Rouen Cathedral, in Notre Dame de Paris,
in Troyes. He was famous all over Europe, and
if we want to find his compositions to-day it is
in the libraries of Italy and France that we must
seek most of them.

Perhaps, then, Dunstable wrote this famous
song, or perhaps some other wrote it. There it
is, at any rate, preserved through the ages, loved
always by a few, though the multitude may know
it not: a great national memorial to a great king
and his greatest victory, as lasting a memorial as
any monument in stone or inscription in brass—

perhaps more so, for who knows whether a great song ever dies?

THE AGINCOURT SONG

A performing version of the Agincourt Song, with piano accompaniment, by Mr. Martin Shaw, will be found in *Songs of Britain,* (Boosey, 2/6).

XXVIII

A GREAT ENGLISHMAN

THE genial Pepys, after a morning in Westminster Hall on a certain Tuesday of February, 1660, a morning spent in watching the excitement of the readmission of the secluded Members of Parliament and the consequent reconstruction of the Long Parliament, went to dinner with one of the members. In the afternoon he was back again in the Hall, and here he met two friends, drawn like himself by a desire for sightseeing. Let him tell the story in his own words :—

" Here I met with Mr. Lock and Pursell, Master of Musique, and went with them to the Coffee House, into a room next the water, by ourselves, where we spent an hour or two till Captain Taylor came and told us that the House had voted the gates of the City to be made up again, and the members of the City that are in prison to be set at liberty; and that Sir G. Booth's case be brought into the House to-morrow. Here we had variety of brave Italian and Spanish songs, and a canon for eight voices,

which Mr. Lock had lately made on these words:
' Domine salvum fac Regem.' Here out of the
windows it was a most pleasant sight to see the
City from one end to the other with a glory
about it, so high was the light of the bonfires,
and so thick round the City, and the bells rang
everywhere."

` Leaving some of the allusions to be explained
by the reader's own recollections of the history of
his country at this crisis in her affairs, the important point is that here we meet with the first
reference to the father of Henry Purcell, our
greatest British composer. The events of the day
of this friendly meeting were of great importance
to him and to his family, and the rejoicings by
bell and by bonfire may well have awakened a
response in his heart, for the coming Restoration,
thus celebrated in advance by the populace at
large and in a special way by this little party of
musical friends, meant congenial and not unpro-
fitable employment for himself and his brother
Thomas, and also, at a later date, for the child
at home, then only a few months old.

It was thus at an historic moment that Henry
Purcell was born. The circumstance of the appearance of our greatest British musician at the
turn of the political tide is notable on account of
its influence on his activities. Much of his work
was to be done within the walls of the reborn national Church, or in the service of the restored
Royal Family; as for his connection with the

theatrical life of the capital, though this would
not have been impossible under the conditions of
the later Protectorate, it could hardly have been
so important a feature of his musical and professional life as it actually became.

II

In the year of his father's death Purcell became
a member of the choir of the Chapel Royal—one
of the " Children of the Chapel." The Chapel
Royal has always been a great nursery of
musicians, and Purcell's youthful position in it
is of importance because it brought him under
the control of three teachers whose guidance and
example were of much value. These were Cooke,
Humphreys and Blow, each of whom occupied in
turn the position of " Master of the Children."
Cooke died in 1672, in Purcell's thirteenth or fourteenth year. He was then succeeded by Humphreys, who died two years later, and was in turn
followed by Blow. On account of their influence
upon Purcell they merit some attention here, but
for the moment nothing more can be said than
that Cooke was himself an old Chapel Royal choir
boy under Charles I, who had later fought for
his master in battle, and was consequently able
to style himself Captain Cooke; that Humphreys
had been sent by Charles II to France to study,
and that in his early death the world lost a potential Mozart; and that Blow was a high-minded and

capable musician who actually gave up his own organist's post at Westminster Abbey to his pupil, Purcell, resuming it on the latter's death.

III

Between the family of the Purcells in England and the contemporary family of the Bachs in Germany an interesting parallel may readily be drawn. Both families were intensely musical, and in both cases the period of musical activity extended over several generations. In the case of the Bachs this activity lasted for more than two centuries, in that of the Purcells for about one-and-a-half. Henry Purcell, like John Sebastian Bach, was but the climatic point in the artistic evolution of his line. The fire of genius began to glow in the generation of his father and uncle, it shot up to incredible heights in that of himself and his brother, and sank slowly in those of his son and his grandson; in the fifth generation it was extinct. The Purcells, like the Bachs, were a galaxy of stars, but in each case the brilliance of a bright, particular star has paled the others into insignificance.

The impression that Henry Purcell made upon the men of his own day and generation is best realised after a reading of the touching and beautiful poem of his friend and collaborator, Dryden. It fittingly records the sad loss which befell our nation by the death of her greatest musician in his thirty-seventh year.

ON THE DEATH OF MR. PURCELL

Mark how the lark and linnet sing;
    With rival notes
They strain their warbling throats
    To welcome in the Spring
    But in the close of night,
When Philomel begins her heavenly lay,
    They cease their mutual spite,
    Drink in her music with delight
    And, listening, silently obey.

So ceased the rival crew, when Purcell came,
They sang no more, or only sung his fame;
Struck dumb, they all admired the godlike man:
    Alas! too soon retired,
    As he too late began,
We beg not hell our Orpheus to restore:
    Had he been there,
    Their sovereign's fear
Had sent him back before.
The power of harmony too well they knew.
He long ere this had tuned their jarring sphere,
    And left no hell below.

The heavenly choir, who heard his notes from high,
Let down the scale of music from the sky:
    They handed him along,
And all the way he taught, and all the way they sung.
Ye brethren of the lyre, and tuneful voice,
Lament his lot; but at your own rejoice:
    Now live secure, and linger out your days;
    The gods are pleased alone with Purcell's lays,
    Nor know to mend their choice.

PURCELL AS CHURCH MUSICIAN

It is as a Church composer that Purcell is known to many. This is but natural, since his time was so largely occupied with the duties of an organist.

At twenty-two he held this position at Westminster Abbey; at twenty-four he became, in addition, organist of the Chapel Royal.

The atmosphere of the latter place is most evidently reproduced in his anthems and " services." What was that atmosphere? A little reflection will convince us that it could not be a very invigorating one, devotionally considered. Nominally a Protestant, Charles was, of course, actually a Romanist. At the best, therefore, the services of his Royal Chapel could make little appeal to him. Moreover, it is inconceivable that so pronounced an evil-liver could have felt any glow of real religious fervour even in a service in keeping with his convictions. We are not, then, to look for great seriousness or depth of feeling in the music provided by royal command. What we do find is a brightness of rhythm and a melodiousness of phrase that must have kept the sovereign in good humour. These were the qualities he prized. The solid woven fabric of the contrapuntal school of British music (a school which had reached its highest point in the days of Queen Elizabeth) were not for him. He had been brought up in France, and the lightness of touch of Lully and the other composers about the French Court was what he desired. Hence he sent one of his first choirboys, young Pelham Humfrey, to France to study, and he became on his return the master of little Henry Purcell. So came the French element into the music of our English Church.

Purcell's anthems are all in many sections—

short sections often lasting only a few moments each. There may be a brief solo, a trio, another solo, another trio, and so forth, until the whole is wound up with a tiny chorus. This last is more often than not an " Alleluia "—a word of praise that Charles must, presumably, have often had upon his lips, since his chief musician shows so great a fondness for it. One feature of these anthems must not be forgotten—the instrumental movements. Charles had been an exile at the French Court, and had often enjoyed the performances of Louis the Fourteenth's band of four-and-twenty fiddlers—the " vingt-quatre violons du Roi." He formed a similar band at his own Court, when at last he possessed one, and, for it, Purcell wrote long introductions and interludes to the anthems. Any reader who wishes to see a specimen of his usual style might get the " Bell Anthem " (so-called), *Rejoice in the Lord Alway* (Novello, 2d.). But in any modern edition of Purcell's anthems he will be misled by the fact that instrumental introductions and interludes have been greatly curtailed, or omitted.

Occasionally Purcell really attained a sincere and religious mood. *Thou knowest, Lord* (Novello, 2d.), is a case in point. It was written for the funeral of Queen Mary, and shortly afterwards sung at the composer's own funeral. Both these events took place in Westminster Abbey, and at every choral funeral in that place since then, *Thou knowest, Lord,* has been sung.

PURCELL'S KEYBOARD MUSIC

The amateur pianist is in my mind as I write the last section of this chapter, and devote it to the keyboard works of Purcell. The theatre works, the many Odes, and the chamber music, must be neglected here.

Of course, there was no piano in Purcell's day, and his works, now published for that instrument, were actually written for the harpsichord, an instrument in appearance not unlike a grand piano, but of which the strings were plucked instead of hammered. Fortunately, there are several very handy small collections of some of the favourite harpsichord works of Purcell. Few of these works are difficult, and to any readers who play even moderately can be recommended the volume edited by Pauer (Augener's Edition, 8,300; 2s. net), and the " Ten Pianoforte Pieces," edited by N. P. and W. H. Cummings (Novello, 2s. 6d. net). A few of the pieces in the latter book, by the way, were originally written for instruments other than the harpsichord, and have been re-arranged by the editors.

The Suite is the most common form used by Purcell. As in the anthem, so here, he makes one long piece by stringing together a number of short ones. Probably he begins with a Prelude, follows this with an " Almand," this, in turn, by a " Courant," this by a " Saraband," and so on. Here, again, is internationalism, the

" Almand " being originally a German dance, the
" Courant " a French one, and the " Saraband "
a Spanish one. The Elizabethan composers had
written suites very much of this character. Those
of Purcell are, however, more developed in character, and there is a sureness of touch with him
that the earlier school, with its less experience of
instrumental style, lacked.

XXIX

A FRENCH MASTER OF MUSIC

WHEN, in 1890, the sixty-eight-year-old César Franck, struck down in the street by the pole of an omnibus, lay dying in his house in Paris, he little realised that in a few short years he would be recognised everywhere as the regenerator of French music. A modest, hard-working organist and music-teacher, caring nothing for glory but a great deal for religion and for art, he plodded through a commonplace working life, doing with his might whatsoever his hand found to do, and leaving to the devoted band of young musicians who formed a brilliant group of pupils any re-criminations as to the small appreciation his genius received from the public or from the profession of which he was a member.

To-day Franck's compositions are everywhere performed, and our own country is by no means behind others in its appreciation of works at once so firmly founded on tradition and so original in character. M. Vincent d'Indy and the group of French musicians who surround him must feel very happy as they survey the results of the ardent propaganda to which their discipleship has led them.

B

A Belgian born, César Franck commenced his artistic education in the music school at Liège. His father destined him for the concert platform, and this prompted a removal to Paris when the boy was twelve years old.

For one hundred and thirty years the Paris Conservatoire has dominated music in the French capital. Generally speaking, its policy has been a cautious one, and it has never been famous for the immediate acceptance of new ideas or for startling innovations. Frequently its professors have lingered in the academic rut when their more talented pupils were longing to discover roads which should lead them to " fresh woods and pastures new." Berlioz, in his memoirs, has much that is amusing to relate as to the conservatism of this institution, and its slow acceptance of Beethoven's works may be taken as a reliable indication of its mental attitude in the old days. The story of Franck's connection with the Conservatoire is interesting. For five years he was a student there. Then for thirty years it gave him no recognition. In 1872, however, by some unexplained intervention on the part of the Minister of Fine Arts, Franck became Professor of the Organ, and for the eighteen years of his life that remained he held this position.

Both as pupil and professor Franck was the subject of misunderstanding and jealousy. In the former capacity he was altogether too original for the steady-going, old-fashioned people who controlled affairs. He seems, decidedly, to have shown some eccentricity in the competitions which form an important annual feature of the life. At fourteen, competing for the piano prize, he took it into his head to play the sight-reading test in the key of a third below, and performed this feat without mistake or hesitation. At nineteen, required to extemporise a fugue and a piece in sonata form as a part of the test for the organ prize, he took the subjects given him for each and treated them simultaneously. Wonderful as these doings might be, they were not according to rule, and it is, perhaps, to the credit of the examiners that in the one case they created a special prize as a consolation for the disqualification the candidate had brought upon himself, and that in the other case they awarded him, at any rate, the second prize.

That Franck should have received so little respect from his colleagues during the period of his professorship will remain a standing disgrace to . them. When a special first performance of *The Beatitudes* was arranged at his house, the Minister of Fine Arts and the Directors of the Conservatoire and the Opera, whose convenience in the selection of date had been carefully consulted, sent excuses. When the Minister of Fine Arts, repentant, tried to get for Franck the additional appointment of Professor of Composition at the Conservatoire, he failed to carry his point against the ill-will of the other members of the Committee. Jules Garcin, the conductor of the Société des Concerts du Conservatoire, had to be very persistent before, in 1889, he could prevail upon the members of his orchestra to perform the magnificent Symphony, and when performed it failed to win any admiration from the authorities. " That a symphony ! " said one of the professors to M. Vincent d'Indy, " Who ever heard of writing for the *cor anglais* in a symphony ? Just mention a single symphony of Haydn or Beethoven introducing the *cor anglais !*" Worst of all, when the composer was laid to rest in an out-of-the-way corner of the cemetery of Montrouge, no representative of the institution, of which he had been, all unrealised, the brightest ornament, accompanied the procession of mourners. Ambrose Thomas, the Director, took to his bed rather than compromise himself in this way, and other professors pleaded indisposition—such, at all events, is M. d'Indy's startling accusation.

Religion counted for a great deal in the life of Franck—the religion of Rome. And his art, like his religion, was founded on tradition. Leaving on one side the seductive paths in which Wagner had led the way, he stepped right back to the early eighteenth century and steeped himself in the spirit of Bach. Then Beethoven threw his mantle upon him, and there are not wanting those who look upon him as the Elisha predestined to carry on the work of the prophet at whose feet he had sat. By drawing the younger French school of his day from paths that for them would have led nowhere, by showing them that the old methods and the classical symphonic style were by no means exhausted, but were yet capable of infinite development, by the exhibition of a sincerity and artistic rectitude the equal of those of the two great masters he followed, by the patient teaching he gave to the earnest students who gathered round him—by all these things, as well as by the attraction of a lovable personality, Franck won the admiration of those who really cared for the welfare of French music, and became a link in the great chain of musical progress.

XXX

A MODERN RUSSIAN COMPOSER

"Not peace but a sword" seems a condition of progress—in art as in life. The eighteenth century had its wars of the Gluckists and Piccinists, the nineteenth of its pro-Wagnerites and anti-Wagnerites. Every great composer has in his time been a storm centre, though not the clearing away of every storm in the musical sky has revealed a great composer. In these present days the storms rage most fiercely, perhaps, around the heads of the three S.'s of the most modern music—Schönberg, Scriabin, and Stravinsky. Here are men who have apparently cast aside all the accepted canons of musical art and evolved, each in his own way (and all the ways very different), something "new and strange." Will their works, which now arouse so much opposition, become at last accepted as ordinary items of the world's répertoire—as those of Strauss, for instance? Or will they at last be cast aside as the product of the aberration of disordered brains (for madness and genius are said to be separated one from another by a very thin party-wall)? Or, worse still, will the world at last quietly bury these com-

posers as the mere notoriety-hunters of a day,
trading on the desire of a bored and blasé society
for something to make its flesh creep?

With Stravinsky I recently had the pleasure of
passing several hours, and he very kindly sub-
mitted himself to a kind of explanatory catechism,
by means of which I endeavoured to search the
recesses of his mind and provide myself with some
account of his decidedly unusual psychology for
the benefit of British readers.

Before I saw Stravinsky a friend described him
to me as follows: "You might take him for a
respectable and intelligent local preacher." Now,
without making any reflection upon the respect-
ability or intelligence either of Stravinsky or the
devoted class of men alluded to by my friend, I
must say that I found the comparison inadequate;
perhaps its foundation lies no deeper than the possession on the part of the composer of a modest
demeanour, the appearance of perfect sincerity,
and—a suit of solemn black. He is of middle
height and somewhat slightly built, has none of
the external signs of a musician (on his head, for
instance), and in conversation displays a frankness
and fullness of expression that, to the interviewer,
at any rate, are very welcome. He was born in
1882, and married in 1906, and his hostages to
fortune already amount to four. For the-most
part he spends his time, as so many of his famous
compatriots have done, on the shores of Lake
Geneva. Here, with his wife and children and a
little party of local musical friends, he lives a

quietly happy life, disturbed only by occasional
rushes to the capital cities of Europe when the
first performances of his works take place.

With Stravinsky, music is an inheritance, for
his father was for long employed in St. Petersburg
as a solo singer at the Court. Apparently personal inclination or parental intention did not at
first lie in a musical direction, for until the age of
twenty, or thereabouts, classical and legal studies
occupied the growing mind. Yet from the age of
nine a remarkable ability as pianist had been recognised in and around the family circle, and the
teaching of a pupil of Rubinstein had been called
in to direct this. In composition and orchestration
Stravinsky is a pupil of Rimsky-Korsakoff.

Only eight years ago did the composer finally
cast aside other pursuits and give himself entirely
to music, and it was the performance of his
Scherzo Fantastique at St. Petersburg, two years
later, that first gave him a position in the
art world of Russia. Paris became a second father-
land to him from 1911, when the ballet *Petrouch-
ka*, described as " burlesque scenes in four pictures," created a furore of admiration. His reputation as a bold innovator became established so
recently as 1913, with the performance of the ballet
Le Sacre du Printemps. The mixed opinions
this received in England when the boards of Drury
Lane received it are still fresh in one's mind.
Since then the same place has witnessed the performance of *The Nightingale*. I believe that
I myself chanced to be the first British writer to

publish any description of this work—a task which
I was better able to perform since I formed one of
a party of friends to whom the composer played
the whole work, partly from proof and partly from
manuscript, and, further, because before its public
performance, he honoured me with a very full
personal explanation of it. In the hope that this
country has not seen the last of a very original
piece of musical-dramatic art, I give below a short
sketch of it.

II

HANS ANDERSEN'S Tales must be the work of reference for those who wish to prepare themselves
for a hearing of *The Nightingale*. The following brief account of the work will show that
the librettist, Mitoussof, has little changed the
story.

Act I—The Emperor of China has heard of the
wonderful bird, the fame of whose nightly performances has spread over the world and evoked
from admirers a whole library of praise ere he and
his self-contained and self-satisfied court have even
heard of them. As the scene opens we see the
courtiers delegated by the Emperor making their
way through the forest to convey to the nightingale
the Imperial command to appear at court. The
little kitchen-maiden, who, alone of all the palace,
has ever heard the bird, leads the way to the tree
where it is to be found. The place is reached, the

nightingale's song is heard, and the command is given and accepted. There follows, as entr'acte, a shadow dance, which Stravinsky calls "Les Courants d'Air." By and by, the Court Chamberlain appears, and drives away the dancers. Then commences a wonderful Chinese march, making large use of the Chinese (pentatonic) scale, and——

Act II opens in the palace with the appearance of a procession, with the august figure of the Emperor, over whose head are held no less than five umbrellas. He and the personages of his court take their places, and the nightingale, perched on the golden stick provided, bursts into song. The Emperor is ravished, and the court ladies sip their tea and attempt by a sort of gargling process to imitate the bird. Then appears an embassy. The Emperor of Japan has sent to the Emperor of China an artificial nightingale, whose little body, covered with diamonds, throws into deep shadow the simple brown of the real one. The artificial bird is wound up, and gives forth its song, and, amidst the tumultuous applause which follows, the real nightingale flies away to its forest through the open window. The mechanical nightingale wins greater favour than the live one. Again the ladies take tea into their mouths and attempt the song. The Emperor appoints the newcomer Imperial Court Nightingale, and, in a fit of fury, formally banishes the real one from his realm.

Act III—The stage is divided into two parts. At the front is an antechamber; beyond it the bedroom of the Emperor. The curtain which divides the two is drawn aside, and we see the Emperor lying there. Upon the bed sits the pale figure of Death, with banner and sword. The Conscience of the Emperor is uneasy, and (represented by a contralto placed in the orchestra) sings its contrition for much wrong-doing. Then the nightingale (the real one) appears. He sings of the Garden of Death. Death listens and begs him to continue. A bargain is made: The nightingale shall sing till daybreak, and Death will then leave the Emperor. By-and-bye, as dawn comes, Death disappears; the Emperor feels strength flowing back as the song continues. He begs the singer to stay always in the palace, but is promised instead a nightly return and a nightly song. The nightingale flies away and a funeral march is heard. Two pages appear and close the curtain before the bed-chamber. The courtiers assemble in the ante-chamber. They have come to see the dead body of their Emperor. The curtains part in the middle, and, as all fall on their faces, the Emperor greets his astonished courtiers with "Good-day!"

Such is the simple plot of this little work, but two or three explanations may be added. First, the difficult song of the real nightingale is taken by a soprano placed in the orchestra. At Drury Lane the illusion was a good deal spoilt by the fact that she was visible to the audience. Second, the song of the mechanical bird is taken by one of the instruments of the orchestra (I think the oboe). Third, a most important part, not referred

to above, is allotted to one of the simple fishermen, who, as Andersen recounts, gather night
after night on the edge of the water to listen to
the song of the nightingale. His voice is heard
after each act, plaintively and poetically comment-
ing on what has gone and foretelling what is to
come. As an instance, I may mention the final
scene of all: here, after all is over on the stage,
the voice of the fisherman is heard telling us that
all that has passed is at the command of the great
celestial spirit, and warning us always to listen to
the birds, for they are the voice of Heaven.
Whether librettist or composer originated this idea
of using one of Andersen's fishermen as "chorus"
I do not know, but the idea is most effectively applied.

The three acts are only of ten to fifteen minutes
duration apiece, and the whole work only lasts forty
minutes. It was begun in 1909, I believe, and
then relinquished for a time. In 1913 its completion was commissioned for the opening of a
new theatre in Moscow. Paris and London, however, as events turned out, had prior performances.
Now in the interval between the beginning of the
work and its completion Stravinsky's style has
completely changed, and he tells me that one of
his chief difficulties has lain in this circumstance.
He says that he tried to continue the work in the
older style, and that where differences are found
they must be taken as the result of unconscious
forces which are too strong for him.

XXXI

MACDOWELL FOR THE PIANIST

WHY is MacDowell not better known in this country? Of course, he is loved by hundreds of musicians and musical people, but I have lately come to the conclusion that there is a big class of music lovers still waiting to have their attention called to him. That class is the amateur pianist class—the better type of amateur pianist, with fingers of some moderate flexibility and a taste for what is good and lasting rather than for what is trivial and ephemeral. Let me first give a very brief sketch of the career of the composer, and then suggest a few works through which acquaintance with him might most suitably be made.

The life of Edward MacDowell was a happy one with a sad ending. He was born in New York in 1861, and died there in 1908. The happiness consisted in the congeniality of his surroundings during a large part of his life, in a considerable measure of appreciation, and, above all, in the help and sympathy that came from his marriage. The sadness lay in some disputes that embittered the last years of his life, and in the unexpected brain failure that finally made him such a pathetic figure.

After piano study as a boy with Teresa Carreño and some other fine pianists at that time in America, MacDowell came to Europe in 1876, at the age of fifteen. He entered the Paris Conservatoire, where he gained much advantage from the piano teaching of Marmontel. The composition teaching there he also found good, on the whole, but, in after life, he used strong language about the useless task of transposing all of Bach's forty-eight preludes and fugues, a labour which consumed months with a very slight return in the way of increase of musical ability. The French musical thought of the time he felt to be, on the whole, rather superficial (apparently the serious-minded Franck-d'Indy group were outside his circle, their connection with the Conservatoire " set " being slight).

Leaving Paris, MacDowell found pleasant surroundings at Wiesbaden, where he worked with Ehlert, Heymann, and, above all, Raff. A short period as chief piano teacher at the Conservatoire at Darmstadt followed, and then came the residence at Frankfort and Wiesbaden, and the marriage to his former pupil, Marian Nevins who survives him, and now devotes her life to unselfish efforts to promote the causes in which he was interested, and especially the welfare of American musicians.

In 1895 MacDowell returned to America. For some years Boston was his home, and he became the centre of a group of active-minded artistic people there. Then, in a misguided moment, he accepted the post of Professor of Music at Colum-

bia University, New York.   Here vexations occurred, and after nine years' tenancy of the post,
he resigned, to be stricken shortly after with the
hopeless malady to which allusion has been made.

All MacDowell's friends (and I have met a number of them, in Europe and America) describe him
as a lovable man, with the highest ideals and a
poetic mind.   The last is evident almost everywhere in his music, and in addition in a slender
volume of poems, collected and published, I believe, after his death.

The immediate appeal that MacDowell's works
make to so many people once they meet with them
is due in part to the fact that they are avowedly
"suggestive music," to use the composer's own
term—that is, they are not so many *Sonatas*,
or *Etudes*, or *Preludes*, but (in most cases)
embody in music the emotions aroused in the composer by some external object or event.

Thus we find such titles for his sets of pieces
as *Forest Idylls, Idylls after Goethe, Poems after
Heine, Marionettes, Woodland Sketches, Sea
Pieces, Fireside Tales,* and *New England Idylls.*
There is no doubt that a large public exists
that likes to have a background to its
music.   It enjoys sound better if it can associate it, in imagination, with sight.   That
is one reason for the wide popularity of so much
of Schumann and of Grieg.   To some people the
very word "sonata" is repellant, and they de-
serve sympathy rather than condemnation, despite
their partial development.

The main thing in making acquaintance with MacDowell is to shun the earlier works, at **any** rate at first. Like other composers, this **one** took a little time to grow an individuality, and the real MacDowell-self is not to be found fully expressed before (say) Opus 45. There are musicians who slight MacDowell because they have only met him in his earlier works, where the influence of his masters outbalanced his originality.

In the list of MacDowell's Piano Works which follows I have merely added a few remarks that may be helpful to the player of MacDowell or to the would-be player wanting a little guidance in the choice of his music.

This I want to say. In going through the works again, with a view to this list, I have been more and more impressed with the fact that I have previously rated MacDowell too low. He is a bigger man than in my littleness of vision I had realised. There is nothing so instructive with regard to a composer as to go carefully through his works in chronological order.

I. THE EUROPEAN PERIOD

FIRST MODERN SUITE, Op. 10. Published 1883.

> 1. *Praeludium;* 2. *Presto;* 3. *Andantino and Allegretto;* 4. *Intermezzo;* 5. *Rhapsody.*

This is not only the " First Modern Suite," but the " first " in several other ways.

It is the first piece the composer thought worthy of preservation, all previous to it being deliberately destroyed.

It and the Second Modern Suite were the first pieces published, Liszt having recommended them to Breitkopf & Härtel.

Two of its movements were probably the first pieces publicly performed in England, MacDowell's early teacher, Mme. Carreño, playing them at an " American Concert " in London, March, 1885.

The composer himself played three movements on his first public appearance in America—at a Kneisel Quartet Concert in Boston, November, 1888.

The " Programme " principle appears in MacDowell's work so early as this first printed piece, for two of the movements have mottoes—from Virgil and Dante.

The foregoing facts are of historical interest, but the music, truth to tell, has a very " early " feeling about it—good as it is of its kind.

PRELUDE AND FUGUE, Op. 13. Published 1883.

SECOND MODERN SUITE, Op. 14. Published 1883.

> 1. *Praeludium;* 2. *Fugato;* 3. *Rhapsody;* 4. *Scherzino;* 5. *March;* 6. *Fantastic Dance.*

It will be noted that some of the historical remarks on the *First Modern Suite* apply also to this. So does the criticism.

M

The *Second Modern Suite* was composed largely in the train, MacDowell at this period spending twelve hours weekly in travelling in order to give lessons to certain little counts and countesses in a mediaeval castle at Erbach-Fürstenau.

Here again appears the " programme " principle, the " Praeludium " being suggested by lines from Byron's *Manfred.*

SERENATA, Op. 16.   Published 1883.

This has a charming little quiet melody, with a *quasi* guitar accompaniment.   There is a brief brilliant middle section, after which the quiet melody returns. It is not great music, but very pleasing.

Two FANTASTIC PIECES, Op. 17.   Published 1884.

1. *Legend; 2. Witches' Dance.*

The second of these pieces is the one of MacDowell's works best known to many school girls.   Both pieces, like much of the work of this period, are good second-hand Raff—the composer's personality not yet having worked to the surface through the influence of his master.

MacDowell himself, in later years, disliked the *Hexentanz* (*Witches' Dance*); yet, as a matter of fact, its popularity is fully justified, taking it for what it is—a bright piece of *salon* music.

Two COMPOSITIONS, Op. 18.   Published 1884.

1. *Barcarolle; 2. Humoresque.*

FOREST IDYLLS, Op. 19.   Published 1884.

1. *Forest Stillness; 2. Play of the Nymphs; 3. Revery; 4. Dance of the Dryads.*

Still no great individuality, but the poetic idea more strongly pronounced, and the nature-worship growing.

Just after writing these words comes the following beautiful sonnet from Mr. Joshua Bannard. He calls it *An Impression (MacDowell's " Forest Stillness," Op.* 19) :—

> The deep'ning shadows steal across the moor,
> The sun is low : and from yon distant brake
> A blackbird sings its parting note : while o'er
> The stillness of the mist-enchanted lake
> Come bleatings from the folds. The rooks about
> The tree-tops fly, and up the dark'ning hill
> The ploughman plods for home. The stars come out
> One after one—and everything is still.
>
> When day and night and heaven and earth are one,
> And all is hushed into tranquility—
> The thoughts that come are thoughts of things undone :
> For twilight is a deep'ning mystery
> Which brings to us when Nature's rest is won
> A sense of God and Immortality.

It is interesting to see that the *Forest Idylls* are dedicated to Marian Nevins—later to become Marian MacDowell.

FOUR COMPOSITIONS, Op. 24. Published 1887.

> 1. *Humoresque;* 2. *March;* 3. *Cradle Song;* 4. *Czardas.*

The Czardas is a brilliant piece of finger work, but pretty conventional.

SIX IDYLLS AFTER GOETHE, Op. 28. Published 1887.

> 1. *In the Woods;* 2. *Siesta;* 3. *To the Moonlight;* 4. *Silver Clouds;* 5. *Flute Idyll;* 6. *The Bluebell.*

These are some of the early fruits of the young Composer's growing reading habit. Goethe and Heine he had devoured and memorised. Like Schumann, he soon showed in his works the joint influences of literature and Nature; indeed almost everything he wrote from this period onward was inspired by something read or something seen—never " absolute " music.

In this case the quotation from Goethe gives a clue to the mood represented, but MacDowell was never a "programmist" in the narrow sense of a composer every detail of whose composition "means something."

SIX POEMS AFTER HEINE, Op. 31.   Published 1887.

1. *From a Fisherman's Hut;* 2. *Scotch Poem;* 3. *From Long Ago;* 4. *The Post Waggon;* 5. *The Shepherd Boy;* 6. *Monologue.*

The remarks made on the preceding apply here also. Mr. Gilman says : " Like the *Idylls after Goethe,* the *Poems after Heine* are devoted to the embodiment of a poetic subject—with the difference that instead of the landscape impressionism of the Goethe studies we have a persistent impulse towards psychological suggestion.   Each of the poems which he has selected has a burden of human emotion, which the music reflects with varying success.   The style is more individualised than in the Goethe pieces, and the invention is, on the whole, on a superior order."

FOUR LITTLE POEMS, Op. 32.   Published 1888.

1. *The Eagle;* 2. *The Brook;* 3. *Moonshine;* 4. *Winter.*

The Eagle is a music-picture prompted by Tennyson's poem-picture—

" He clasps the crag with hooked hands :
Close to the sun in lonely lands,
Ring'd with the azure world he stands.

" The wrinkled sea beneath him crawls ;
He watches from his mountain walls,
And like a thunderbolt he falls."

Represented in terms of tone, that promises something noble.   Play the piece and see whether the promise is realised.   MacDowell was a great Tennyson lover—as others of his works prove.

Winter is a music-picture after Shelley.   It is a shimmering, delicate, and almost Debussy-like piece—without, of course, the Debussyan whole-tone scale.

II. THE AMERICAN PERIOD

ETUDE DE CONCERT, Op. 36.   Published 1889.

"Don't put that dreadful thing on your programme," telegraphed MacDowell to Teresa Carreño, upon seeing an announcement that she was to play for the first time his Concert Study in F♯.

LES ORIENTALES, Op. 37.   Published 1889.

>   1. *Clair de Lune; 2. Dans le Hamac; 3. Danse Andalouse.*

Victor Hugo inspired these pieces.   Speaking of Op. 35, Op. 36, and Op. 37 (the Romance for 'cello and orchestra, the piece just mentioned and the present pieces), Mr. Gilman says : " Perfunctory is the word which one must use to describe the creative impulse of which they are the ungrateful legacy. . . . Perhaps they may be described as almost the only instances in which MacDowell gave heed to the possibility of a reward not primarily and exclusively artistic.   They are sentimental and unleavened, though they are not without a certain rather inexpressive charm."

It seems as though MacDowell was passing through a bad period—as though some weakness had fallen on him suddenly ; some fleeting desire for rapid popularity.

MARIONETTES, Op. 38.   Published as 6 pieces 1888, as 8 pieces 1901.

>   1. *Prologue; 2. Soubrette; 3. Lover; 4. Witch; 5. Clown; 6. Villain; 7. Sweetheart; 8. Epilogue.*

Surely the idea for this scheme came from Schumann.   Here is humour !

The later edition of these pieces is much superior to the earlier.   The Prologue and Epilogue were added.

In these pieces MacDowell first commences to draw upon the wide resources of the English language to express his wishes as to performance, abandoning the limited conventional Italian expressions.

TWELVE STUDIES, Op. 39.   Published 1890.

>   Book I. : 1. *Hunting Song;* 2. *Alla Tarantella;*
>   3. *Romance;* 4. *Arabesque;* 5. *In the Forest;*
>   6. *Dance of the Gnomes.*

>   Book II. : 7. *Idyll;* 8. *Shadow Dance;* 9. *Intermezzo* or *Melody;* 10. *Scherzino;* 11. *Hungarian.*

Mr. Gilman makes an acute distinction between the " imperfectly realised romanticism " of these studies and " the intimate spirit of sincere romance " of many other pieces of the composer.

SONATA TRAGICA, Op. 45.   Published 1893.

The composition of this, the first of the four noble Sonatas, was prompted by the death of MacDowell's old master, Raff.   The Largo was written at a time when the composer was much worried and overworked ; probably he always associated it with a sense of escape from everyday trials, for it remained one of his favourite movements.   Mr. Gilman remarks that in the first three movements there are details of tragedy, whereas the last appears to be a generalisation—" a steadily progressive triumph, which at its close is completely shattered."   Accepting this view, it is natural to regard the last movements as a (partly prophetic) epitome of the composer's own life.

Like the other three Sonatas, this requires a real *dramatic sense* on the part of the player.   Like others of the works it was first heard in the Chickering Hall, Boston, from the hands of MacDowell himself (Kneisel Quartet Concert, March, 1893).

TWELVE VIRTUOSO STUDIES, Op. 46.   Published 1894.
    1. *Novelette;* 2. *Moto Perpetuo;* 3. *Wild Chase;* 4. *Improvisation;* 5. *Elfin Dance;* 6. *Valse Triste;* 7. *Burleske;* 8. *Bluette;* 9. *Träumerei;* 10. *March Wind;* 11. *Impromptu;* 12. *Polonaise.*

That the *real* MacDowell is emerging, now that the opus forties have been arrived at, is evident in the very first harmonies of the very first piece here (*Novelette*).   The *Polonaise* is a stirring piece of good salon music, influenced by Chopin.

AIR AND RIGAUDON, Op. 49.   Published 1894.

SECOND SONATA (" EROICA "), Op. 50.   Published 1895.

Here is an Arthurian work, the result of that early devotion to Tennyson already alluded to.   Pianists who wish to put themselves in the spirit of the work should soak for some weeks in *Idylls of the King*.   A volume might be written on the influence of the Arthurian legends upon literature, painting and music, and MacDowell enrolled himself among a noble company when he brought forth his contribution to the subject.

That the mature MacDowell has not yet appeared we find at once in the first movement, where there are glorious themes but occasional figures of accompaniment that depart little from conventionality, and short stretches of something approaching mere passage work.   Nevertheless the movement is a wonderfully fine one.

The second movement, a *Scherzo*, is founded on a picture which, in its turn, was based on a poem.   (So the three arts inter-relate!) The picture is one by Doré. These lines give the clue.

> Next morning, while he passed the dim-lit woods,
> Himself beheld three spirits mad with joy
> Come dashing down upon a tall wayside flower,
> Which shook beneath them as the thistle shakes
> When the gray linnets wrangle for the seeds.

But if the composer was inspired to write the movement by Doré's picture illustrating Tennyson's " spirits mad with joy," in it he has, apparently, summed up the general impression of the whole long passage beginning, " The land was full of signs," and ending,

> " So glad were spirits and men
> Before the coming of the sinful Queen."

The third movement is haunting. The composer said, " It was suggested by my idea of *Guinevere.*"

The fourth movement, representing the Passing of Arthur, seems the most clearly and unmistakably " programmatic " of any.

The Sonata is exhausting to play—physically and mentally. MacDowell himself found it so.

WOODLAND SKETCHES, Op. 51. Published 1896.

> 1. *To a Wild Rose;* 2. *Will-o'-the-Wisp;* 3. *At an old Trysting Place;* 4. *In Autumn;* 5. *From an Indian Lodge;* 6. *To a Water Lily;* 7. *From Uncle Remus;* 8. *A Deserted Farm;* 9. *By a Meadow Brook;* 10. *Told at Sunset.*

Here are products of nature-communion on the " farm " at Peterboro. Riding, driving, and " pretending to hunt " (as the neighbours called it, for Macdowell hated to take life), the composer revelled in an out-of-doors existence. Flower-love comes into Nos. 1 and 6, and it may be recalled that he had a tenderness, amounting to affection, towards the flower-world. It hurt MacDowell, for instance, if his wife watered some of the plants in the garden and not others !

Here we find MacDowell's " suggestive music " (as

he called it—preferring the term to " programme music " for his compositions) approaching its best. The pianist who has yet to make acquaintance with this composer might do worse than let these pieces make the introduction. Occasionally there is a slight- ness of content and of structure that demands careful playing. *To a Wild Rose*, for instance, is near the verge of the commonplace and can easily be pushed over by a player who cannot do it " just right." *In Autumn*, again, has a rather weak middle section, otherwise it is a most jolly piece, reminiscent of days when there is just enough frost in the air to invigorate. *At an old Trysting Place* is not strong. The brilliant little *Will-o'-the-Wisp* fully justifies its taking title. As regards *From Uncle Remus*, see the remarks later, under *Fireside Tales*.

SEA PIECES, Op. 55. Published 1898.

> 1. *To the Sea; 2. From a Wandering Iceberg; 3. A.D. 1620; 4. Starlight; 5. Song; 6. From the Depths; 7. Nautilus; 8. In Mid-Ocean.*

Of all his short pieces MacDowell preferred these, and I think he was right. Nos. 1, 6 and 8 were special favourites with him. Here we find him at last on his highest level—so far, at any rate, as his shorter works are concerned. The snatches of poetry prefixed are MacDowell's own (as is the case in the *New England Idylls,* and others of the later piano works).

Concerning *To the Sea*, Gilman says, " It is but thirty-one bars long, yet within this limited frame he has confined a tone-picture which for breadth of con- ception and concentrated splendour of effect is par- alleled in the contemporary literature of the piano only by himself." The shimmering lights of the Iceberg, in No. 2, are reflected in a series of harmonies which seem to justify the rarely-remembered origin of the word " chromatic."

Some time ago a reader of *The Music Student* raised the question of the metronome rate given in the case of *Nautilus,* and it was agreed by Messrs. Elkin that this should probably be 84 (*not* 54).

In Mid-Ocean is a piece of noble tone painting.

THIRD SONATA ("NORSE"), Op. 57.   Published 1900.

As the *Sea Pieces* mark the attainment of a new level in the shorter works, so, I think, does this *Norse Sonata* mark a new level in the longer ones. Personally, I prefer it to the *Keltic Sonata,* which followed, but here I have the composer himself and a number of his admirers against me. Both works were, by the way, dedicated to Grieg. It is surprising to find the mind which conceived the perfect daintiness of some of the short pieces capable of the force of the Sonatas, and especially of the last two. In the works of the period we have now reached, there is freshness of outlook and an individuality in every turn of expression. (The harmonies, never forced, are very personal, for instance, and there are little tricks and turns of melody, such as what may be called the MacDowellian-Scotch-Snap), which on every page labels the music with its creator's name.

About five years separated the composition of the Second and Third Sonatas, and the development in the meantime has been great. In the Third there is never a note of padding—everything is vital. The movements are bound to one another by a community or relationship of material and become a whole.

The motto lines at the head of the first page are again the composer's own, and serve to give the spirit of the work. "Night had fallen on a day of deeds" says the Poet-Composer, and he goes on to imagine

> "A Skald's strong voice
> With tales of battles won;
> Of Gudrun's love,
> And Sigurd, Siegmund's son."

To breathe the atmosphere of the piece before playing it, read the text of Wagner's *Siegfried* and *Dusk
of the Gods,* or (better still) the gory *The Fall of the
Nibelungs* (translated by Margaret Armour, " Everyman's Library," 1/- net), or even better again (because giving the more Northern version of the legends), the *Völsunga Saga* (translated from the Ice-
landic by Magnusson and William Morris, Walter
Scott Co., 1/- net).

FOURTH SONATA (" KELTIC "), Op. 59. Published
1901.

In the subject of its inspiration this work is obviously very nearly akin to the *Norse Sonata.* The atmosphere of the story of Deidré and that of the life
and death of Cuchullin are worked into the substance
of the *Keltic Sonata.* Gael readers may know something of the Cycle of the Red Branch, the collection
of legends whence MacDowell drew his interest in the
tales of his forefathers. *The Coming of Cuchulain*
and some others of the works of Mr. Standish O'Grady
might well be found of service—but these, I am
ashamed to say, I have yet to read.

To my mind the first movement of this work, though
fine, is not so strong as the first movement of the
Norse Sonata. There is no theme in the middle movement that haunts me as some of his themes do. The
last movement is really a brilliant yet often mysterious
Scherzo, and despite its solemn Coda (with references
to the first movement), does not seem to me quite a
fitting finale to the work. This, however, is a purely
personal view, and I hold myself at liberty to change
it at any time when some more enlightened Mac-Dowell-
ite shall give me a convincing exposition of my errors
of judgment. Despite the critics, the *Norse Sonata*
remains my favourite for the moment.

FIRESIDE TALES, Op. 61. Published 1902.

1. *An Old Love Story;* 2. *Of Brer Rabbit;* 3. *From a German Forest;* 4. *Of Salamanders;* 5. *A Haunted House;* 6. *By Smouldering Embers.*

Picking out the plum of humour first of all, let me say, apropos of *Brer Rabbit,* that I hope no reader is unacquainted with the works of Joel Chandler Harris. If there be such a reader let him conceal his shame and immediately buy *Uncle Remus* and *Nights with Uncle Remus* (Routledge, 6d. each). This done, let him play *Of Brer Rabbit* (in the *Fireside Tales*), and *Of Uncle Remus* (in the *Woodland Sketches*), and see if he can identify the passages that were in the Composer's mind when he wrote them. It should not be difficult. MacDowell was fond of the American humorists. Mark Twain he revelled in, and Joel Chandler Harris gave him never-failing delight.

Surely some of MacDowell's walks with his friend Templeton Strong are commemorated in *From a German Forest.*

NEW ENGLAND IDYLLS, Op. 62. Published 1902.

1. *An Old Garden;* 2. *Midsummer;* 3. *Midwinter;* 4. *With Sweet Lavender;* 5. *In Deep Woods;* 6. *Indian Idyll;* 7. *To an Old White Pine;* 8. *From Puritan Days;* 9. *From a Log Cabin;* 10. *The Joy of Autumn.*

MacDowell's music naturally connects itself with one's reading, and pianists who wish to get something of the New England spirit, so that the appeal of these pieces may be the more vivid, might well read Nathaniel Hawthorne, especially perhaps *The Scarlet Letter, Twice Told Tales* (Everyman's Library, each 1/- net), and *Grandfather's Chair.* The last is really a children's book, but it gives a series of sketches of events in the history of New England that are just the thing for the general reader who is not too much grown-up in spirit as well as in body. Then there is the charming little book by M. E. Wilkins, *A Humble Romance* (Douglas, 1/-), with its " Symphony in Lavender," which some may come to connect in thought with MacDowell's lavender music (No. 4 above).   But there is no end to the New England literature, for the North-Eastern states had a long start over the others in the writing of books, and are still at it as actively as ever.

From a Log Cabin recalls the Peterboro hut in which the Composer worked.   Its motto is now inscribed on his memorial tablet—

> " A house of dreams untold,
>   It looks out over the whispering tree-tops
>   And faces the setting sun."

Mr. Gilman says of this piece—" It is steeped in an atmosphere which is felt in no other of his works; is the issue of an inspiration more profoundly contemplative than any to which he had hitherto responded."   All this is true, but, as is so often the case in MacDowell, the player must be a poet !

The *Joy of Autumn* is one of the most brilliant pieces ever written.   It needs good fingers !

THE " EDGAR THORN " PIECES

Some small pieces of MacDowell were published under the pseudonym of " Edgar Thorn."   It is understood that the copyright was given to a nurse, as an acknowledgment of some services she had given. These pieces are as follows :—

IN LILTING RHYTHM (two pieces).

FORGOTTEN FAIRY TALES.

> 1. *Sung outside the Prince's Door; 2. Of a Tailor and a Bear; 3. Beauty in the Rose Garden; 4. From Dwarf Land.*

SIX FANCIES.

1. *A Tin Soldier's Love;* 2. *To a Humming Bird;*
3. *Summer Song;* 4. *Across Fields;* 5. *Bluette;*
6. *An Elfin Round.*

AMOURETTE.

These all show MacDowell on his lighter side. The *Forgotten Fairy Tales* and *Six Fancies* are especially likely to interest children, though not all within the normal childish capacity as regards performance.

THE BACH TRANSCRIPTIONS

SIX LITTLE PIECES OR SKETCHES BY J. S. BACH.

1. *Courante;* 2. *Menuet;* 3. *Gigue;* 4. *Menuet;*
5. *Menuet;* 6. *March.*

Provided the legitimacy of re-writing Bach in modern pianistic style, and with enriched harmonies, be conceded, these pieces must be considered very successful.

Printed in Great Britain by Ebenezer Baylis and Son. Worcester.

Lightning Source UK Ltd.
Milton Keynes UK
UKHW010609120219

337137UK00007B/1467/P